# LIVE GENERATION

## IRAN'S 1999 STUDENT UPRISING THAT OPENED THE DOOR FOR SECULAR DEMOCRACY

### REZA MOHAJERINEJAD

iUniverse, Inc.
NEW YORK   BLOOMINGTON

**Live Generation**
**Iran's 1999 Student Uprising that Opened**
**the Door for Secular Democracy**

*iUniverse books may be ordered through booksellers or by contacting:*

*iUniverse*
*1663 Liberty Drive*
*Bloomington, IN 47403*
*www.iuniverse.com*
*1-800-Authors (1-800-288-4677)*

*Because of the dynamic nature of the Internet, any Web addresses or links contained in this book may have changed since publication and may no longer be valid.*

*ISBN: 978-1-4502-3796-3 (sc)*
*ISBN: 978-1-4502-3797-0 (dj)*
*ISBN: 978-1-4502-3798-7 (ebk)*

*Library of Congress Control Number: 2010908281*

*Printed in the United States of America*

*iUniverse rev. date: 6/10/2010*

*For Dariush Forouhar, Parvaneh Eskandari, Akbar Mohammadi, Ezzat Ibrahim Nejad, and all those who have given their lives for freedom in Iran.*

*And for my grandmother, Ahoo, who passed away just following the completion of the first draft of this book.*

*A special thanks to Dr. Misagh Parsa for his thoughtful input and guidance throughout the life of this project.*

# CONTENTS

# AZADI

An zaman keh benhadam sar beh paye azadi
daste khood ze jan shostam az baraye azadi

ta magar beh dast aram damane vesalash ra
midavam beh paye sar dar ghafaye azadi

dar mohite tofanza maheraneh dar jang ast
nakhodaye estebdad ba khodaye azadi

damane mohabat ra gar koni ze khon rangi
mitavan tora goftan nakhodaye azadi

*- Farrokhi Yazdi*

# Endorsement

Reza Mohajerinejad offers an eloquent, eyewitness account of the courageous student movement that sprang up in July 1999 and its ongoing impact to this day, when its themes of a secular democratic Iran have been embraced by millions in the ongoing Green Movement. Imprisoned, tortured, exiled, but unbowed, his gripping story provides deep and moving insight into the activists, their actions, and thoughts as central protagonists in Iran's long revolutionary history, and its hopeful future.

Dr. John Foran
Professor of Sociology, University of California, Santa Barbara

I have known Mr. Mohajerinejad since 1998. I was regularly in touch with him in the spring and summer of 1999. There is authenticity in his memoirs and recollections of the student movement from those critical months preceding and following the fateful events in July 1999. This is an invaluable book that provides the personal account of one of the student leaders about the founding of student pro-democracy movement as a pivotal event in the contemporary history of Iran.

Dr. Hamid Akbari
Audrey Reynolds Distinguished Teaching Professor of Management
Director, Dr. Mohammad Mossadegh Leadership Fund at Northeastern
Illinois University in Chicago

# FOREWORD

Reza Mohajerinejad's fascinating memoir details the struggles of Iranian students against the Islamic regime, focusing on the six-day uprising of July 1999 that became an epic challenge to the Islamic government nearly two decades after its establishment. During the uprising thousands of students revolted and attacked the regime's economic, political, and ideological foundation. Although Mohajerinejad and many young, secular democrats were arrested, tortured, and some even lost their lives, it is now clear that they were on the forefront of the anti-Islamic Republic conflict that paved the way for the 2009 protests against the denial of political rights to the Iranian people. Indeed, Mohajerinejad and his cohort can be considered the heroes and heroines of the recent struggles for democracy and freedom in Iran.

The protests of Mohajerinejad and other students were rooted in the unresolved conflicts of Iran's revolution of 1979. The revolution was carried out by a broad coalition of actors including students, workers, middle class citizens, Shiite clergy, merchants, shopkeepers, and artisans. Although these collectivities each had their own specific demands and initiated their struggles at different times, towards the end of 1978 in the final phase of the revolutionary struggles, they came together in calling for the overthrow of the monarchy. During the final two days, protestors shouted for "Independence, Freedom, and Islamic Government." Most Iranians expected that an Islamic government would guarantee political freedoms, eliminate arbitrary authority, and inject accountability into the political system. The middle and working classes, in particular, expected an Islamic Republic to eliminate corruption and guarantee social justice and equity in the distribution of wealth and income. However, the vast majority of Iranians never demanded the establishment of a theocracy per se, the repression of dissent, the imposition of harsh cultural restrictions, the execution of homosexuals, or the relegation of women to second-class citizenship.

Students and secular forces initiated the political struggles in 1977, but political repression limited their capacity for mobilization. Under repressive conditions, mosques became safe spaces to mobilize and act collectively. Although most clergy were non-political and did not condone political confrontation, mobilization through the mosques provided an opportunity for a small segment of the clergy to take an active role in the anti-Shah conflict. Ayatollah Khomeini swiftly rose to a position of leadership. During the revolutionary struggles, he repeatedly promised freedom from dictatorship and independence from Western imperialism, and he condemned corruption and the pillaging of national resources. He often declared that an Islamic Republic would guarantee human rights, labor rights, and women's rights. Thus, Khomeini received the backing of the vast majority of the Iranian population.

However, before the Shah's ouster, Khomeini did not openly reveal his radical, theocratic ideology to the Iranian people. In his public statements, he never mentioned doctrinal issues such the concept of jurist's guardianship. To the detriment of Iranians, shortly after returning to Iran after years of exile, Khomeini managed to establish an Islamic theocracy. In Khomeini's theocratic system, power was concentrated in the hands of the clergy and their allies, and everyone was forced to observe a strict Islamic code of conduct. Although many people opposed such a theocracy, ideological and political divisions prevented them from forming a united front against the new regime. Khomeini used three tactics to eliminate opposition. Through external conflicts such as the hostage crisis and the Iraq war, he promoted national cohesion. To undermine the left, he touted material benefits such as free housing, electricity and water that the Islamic Republic promised to the *mostazafin*, the poor and oppressed. Finally, he organized the ruthless Revolutionary Guard and paramilitary forces that repressed dissidents. Between 1981 and 1985, Khomeini's regime killed or executed nearly 12,000 people, almost 4,000 of whom were students.

Khomeini also took the unprecedented step of decreeing the closure of all universities for at least two years while the regime purged them of non-Islamic elements. Repressing dissident student organizations, the regime promoted Islamic associations that served its political and ideological interests and agendas. After Khomini's death, the regime's right-wing faction demanded that Islamic student associations sever all ties with the radical faction of the regime or disband. The order antagonized Islamic students, leading them to support the election of the reformist President Khatami in 1977.

Khatami's attempts at reforms along with reduced political repression provided students an opportunity to act collectively on behalf of expanded civil liberties and political freedom. This was the context within which Mohajerinejad and his fellow students, sparked by the closure of a national newspaper, mobilized against government repression. During the protests, slogans such as "The people are miserable! The clerics are acting like gods!" struck at the heart of the Islamic regime. The protests quickly spread to all major cities with concentrations of college and university students. For six days, Mohajerinejad and his student allies successfully shook the very foundation of the Islamic Republic and demonstrated that the secular movement and aspirations for democracy were still alive.

The government was caught by surprise. The Islamic Republic's rulers had assumed that waves of repression, assassinations and executions had eliminated the secular opposition and insured the regime's grasp on power. The leaders of the regime's competing factions, reformers and conservatives, briefly united and responded with the same repressive measures used earlier. They arrested Mohajerinejad and many other students along with a large number of ordinary people who had joined the protests outside the universities. In the end, repression prevailed, and the people's democratic aspirations were thwarted.

Some of those who had been arrested lost their lives, but most were eventually released from prison, including Mohajerinejad. When I heard he managed to escape to Europe, I contacted him and invited him to Dartmouth College to tell our students about the nature of the student movement in Iran. His visit to my classroom was warmly received, and the college newspaper wrote about his ordeal and covered his views on the conditions in Iran. Later, a group of Dartmouth students organized a panel discussion on student activism and invited him back for a second visit to share his experiences.

A number of us urged Mohajerinejad to write a memoir of these events and, fortunately he agreed. Live Generation Iran's 1999 Student Uprising that Opened the Door for Secular Democracy is a rare document that tells the powerful story of the struggle for freedom by the students and people of Iran in the face of enormous suffering and betrayals. It also reveals much about the nature of the Islamic state and the operation of its coercive apparatus. The book is immensely readable and compels the reader to engaged until the outcome. It is a must for students and scholars interested in Iran, student protests, social movements, and democratization.

Misagh Parsa, PhD
Professor of Sociology
Dartmouth College
Hanover, New Hampshire

# PREFACE

In 1999, I spent 137 days in what was then Iran's most violent prison. I was a political prisoner. What I saw, what I heard, and what I endured in my days of interrogation and torture followed by hours of solitary confinement showed me that the human heart, with its unshakable desire for freedom, is a mighty force. I was a young man when I entered the doors of Tohid. I came from a good family. I loved my country and my people. I loved the history of our ancient past, and I wanted basic human rights for the children of the future of Iran. I left Tohid prison no less certain that what we worked for was not only our right, but that if we were to continue as a country, it was a necessity. I can honestly say that at no time in the darkest moments of physical and emotional pain did I consider giving up. The only way to stop me, and those like me who believe in a secular democracy for our country, is to kill us. Even that, however, leaves our legacy. Someone will remember, and in that, our work lives on.

The hours of solitary confinement would seem from the outside to be a respite from the hours of torture that preceded them. It seems logical that after being interrogated for extended periods, forced to write pages of scenarios from my political past, followed by beatings that took on new levels of cruelty depending on the moods of my captors, that being brought back to my cell would feel like a relief.

In truth, the hours behind the locked door of my cell were the most excruciating. The physical pain, the throbbing of open wounds, became even more intense. The stench of the prison walls was indistinguishable as it mixed with the smells of my own unwashed body, the infected flesh of cuts and bruises that went untreated, and the filth of the cell in which I stayed that had housed so many prisoners before me.

A single light bulb hung from the ceiling. The glare was blinding. It burned twenty-four hours a day, causing days to turn to nights without any real awareness from within my cell. In the first few weeks I was certain every night would be my last. I didn't know who from my group had already been killed, and I was in constant fear for the lives of my family members.

The mind begins to play tricks on anyone suffering from the torture of solitary confinement. Sleep often doesn't come, and the voices in my head would work to calm me before they turned to panic again. Often I dreamed of my life before I was captured, reconstructing every detail of my early life, the sound of my mother's voice, and the way the wind blew the rice fields on my father's land by the Caspian Sea. I would sometimes try to imagine how life would be once I was gone. What my family would do, my friends, how they would go on with their lives.

I rarely dared to think that I might be released. My captors were very clear that I would die in that prison, so imagining the possibility of living on the other side of prison walls was a luxury I seldom allowed myself. What I did allow myself was a promise that should I live to tell the story of what the Islamic Republic had done to its people, I would never stop working for freedom for the people of Iran.

The story of my imprisonment is only important in that it is a reminder to all of us who are outside of prison walls that at this very moment, in Iran and in other places throughout the world, there are human beings who are experiencing the exact same circumstances that I lived through a decade ago. Political prisoners in Iran face the worst kinds of physical and mental torture. They are beaten and raped, threatened and left in solitary confinement until they are on the edge of madness. Yet, even with the threat of all this, citizens of Iran continue their quest for freedom.

On June 12, 2009, the presidential election results handed Mahmoud Ahmadenejad yet another term in the dictatorship led by the Supreme Leader of the Islamic Republic of Iran, Ali Khamanei. There is little doubt both inside and outside of Iran that the vote was fixed, and since the elections people have come out in larger numbers than ever before to protest the results. They have been beaten in the streets by hired militia, shot, sprayed with toxic tear gas, and rounded up in huge numbers to be taken to prisons all over Iran.

What is remarkable about all that we have seen since the elections is that the resistance has continually grown. What started as the "Green Movement" has evolved into what people now refer to as the "Green Revolution." It is clear that the clerics who control the regime have too much at stake should they lose control, and for this reason they continue to resort to unimaginable tactics to control the masses. Yet the fight continues.

I am of a generation that was born before the Islamic Revolution of 1979, but was too young to really remember life before the Islamic Republic of Iran. Our generation had our heads filled with Islamic propaganda at a very early age, our history books rewritten to support the ideology that fit best with Shia Islam. Many of us were children during the Iran-Iraq War. We saw the enormous loss of life that war produced, and all the while, what the Islamic Republic bet on was that we would remain loyal so long as our country was embroiled in war with our enemies.

When the war was over, our generation was left to pick up the pieces. The focus changed, and for perhaps the first time, the truth about our government started coming to light. What we saw was that anyone who disagreed with the Supreme Leader, at that time Ayatollah Khomeini, was in grave danger of being imprisoned and executed by the Islamic Republic.

In 1999, an event occurred that changed the political landscape and the control the Islamic Republic of Iran had over its youth forever. In the middle of the night of July 8, 1999, government-sanctioned thugs attacked the student dormitories of Tehran University. What followed were days of protest that would later come to be known as 18 Tir—a reference to the day of the attacks according to the Persian calendar. The protesters grew in numbers until some fifty thousand students came out against the government of the Islamic Republic of Iran. I was one of the organizers of those protests, and as such became a target for revenge by the regime.

What is worth noting about the protests of 18 Tir is that they represented so much more than mere numbers. In those days, just twenty years after the Islamic Revolution, speaking out against the government in Iran was unheard of. Those who participated were for the most part the young generation. They were unafraid, and they had less to lose. Us standing up against the regime was something the government hadn't really counted on. We knew nothing else but the Islamic Republic, yet somehow the outside world had gotten in. Technology like cell phones, satellite, and the Internet provided knowledge of our basic human rights. History books that excluded the significance of the events of the last forty or fifty years could not stop information from getting into Iran, and in 1999, our generation was truly on fire.

The regime was able to arrest thousands of students following the protest. They were able to keep those of us who organized the protests imprisoned—some of us for many years—but they could not rewrite what happened in July 1999. The protests of 18 Tir happened, and Iranian citizens remembered it even when our voices were silenced in the months that followed. What we did back then cracked the door of freedom open for the first time in twenty years of oppression. People understood that if it was possible for a small number of students to bring fifty thousand others out in opposition to the tyranny of the Islamic Republic of Iran, it was possible to one day bring out one hundred thousand, one million, or more.

What we see in present day Iran is truly the Live Generation. The protesters are taking to the streets at every major event, including the anniversary of 18 Tir, Students Day, the death of Ayatollah Montazeri, and the Islamic day of mourning, *Ashura*. The movement has been pulled together using a grassroots approach that ensures that it isn't top heavy. The candidates who helped spur the movement, Mir Hossein Mousavi and Mehdi Karroubi, are but symbols at this point. The movement, however, is no longer just about the fraudulent elections of 2009. The movement has become what most of us believe will lead to an eventual revolution in Iran. Mousavi and Karroubi represent a reformist idea. That idea is quickly becoming irrelevant as the people of Iran seek true secular democracy and freedom.

*Live Generation* is the story of what led up to 18 Tir, what happened to us, and how it laid the foundation for a new generation of youth that is willing to risk personal freedom, safety, and life itself for freedom for our country. Yet this new generation is not alone. They are today joined by every combination of citizenry of our country. While in

1999 our student movement was largely made up of young people who had the silent support of families and friends, today's protests in Iran include young, old, rich, and poor. While our protests involved major universities in cities all across Iran, today we see not only universities but even conservative bastions of Islamic teachings like Qom and Mashad getting involved.

Although the last year has demonstrated the strength of the opposition to the Islamic Republic of Iran, the dictatorship of the Supreme Leader Ali Khamanei will no doubt continue to use whatever dehumanizing tactics they can to try to suppress our voices. But the Live Generation of a new era will not be suppressed. This book is a tribute to all those brave souls who, like me, cannot forget those who have suffered at the hands of this repressive government. It is for those who have died in the streets, faced unfathomable torture, and have continued to scream from the rooftops night after night the freedom call of the Green Revolution, "Death to the Dictator."

# ACKNOWLEDGMENTS

I have mentioned several key members of the National Union of Iranian Students and Graduates throughout the book. What follows is a list of others who were instrumental in helping in the student movement of the last decade. In the interest of safety, some names have been omitted. These people know who they are and that without their help we might never have set the foundation for the movement that we did.

Hamid Alizadeh
Abdureza Ashrafpour
Ayoub Lorestani Hadizadeh
Farzad Hamidi
Mohammad Hashimi
Mohammad Reza Kasrani
Mehdi Mesbah
Mohsen Sadeghi Nouri
Payman Piran
Mostafa Piran
Keyvan Radbin
Kianoush Sanjari
Kouroush Sehati
Maryam Shansi
Hossein "Aria" Yekta

# CHAPTER 1

# JULY 1999 ... 18 TIR

### JULY 8, 1999, TEHRAN, 2:00 AM

The campus was quiet that Thursday night in early July. Summer in Tehran is hot, and we slept head-to-toe in a cramped dorm room. We were students, political friends, intellectuals in the making, and we were working for secular democracy in Iran.

We woke to the fanatic cries of those who attacked the dorms. They shouted the name of God before landing blows that elicited screams from our fellow students. The sudden, shocking sound of gunshots rang out between the buildings, and the crashing of breaking glass and terror reverberated within the campus walls.

Terrified, we scattered in the chaos. Mayhem followed, hours of violence that can only be likened to a battle scene from a war. From where I hid I watched as they tore apart one of the dorms. One man barked violent orders. I remember his bearded face and the un-tucked shirt he wore. From where I crouched behind a door, I heard the others refer to him as "Haji." He barked out commands that his underlings followed without hesitation. Later I would see a picture of this man and recognize him as Tehran's former police chief, Farhad Nazari.

The Islamic Republic of Iran later acquitted Nazari of any involvement in the attacks. However, too many of us saw him that night. Farhad Nazari was not only involved in the planning, but he was

1

an active participant in the assault on students at Tehran University on July 8, 1999.

As the attacks continued, they became more brutal. We knew they were likely looking for us, or those who sympathized with us. As in any group based on fundamentalist ideology, the Ansar-e Hezbollah feel justified in taking licenses that go far beyond the realm of social justice or human rights. We listened that night as they screamed curses at students in the name of God, crashing into rooms indiscriminately, terrorizing whomever they found behind the dormitory walls. They carried batons, swords, and guns, and there seemed to be anywhere from three to four hundred of them.

I made my way outside to the campus grounds, where I saw students being thrown from buildings three stories high. With each body they flung from the windows, I remember hearing "Ya Zahra," which literally translates as "Accept our sacrifice." Later we heard that the Hezbollah had grabbed students and broken the bones of their arms like tree branches, screaming "Allahu Akbar" (God is great) or "Khamenei Rahbar," indicating support for and from the Islamic Republic's Supreme Leader, Ali Khamenei.

For whatever reason, they were unable to get into Building 17, and the students who stayed there had climbed the stairs to the roof and were throwing objects down, aiming to hit members of the Hezbollah wherever possible. This would mark the beginning of our resistance, and it would last for the next several days.

From where I hid watching, I could see that members of the Hezbollah attacked the students indiscriminately. It didn't matter to them which students they injured or killed. The attacks were not personal per se, but the message they sent was very clear. Our political activities had brought out the wrath of the Islamic Republic authorities. They were declaring that they had control, and enough was enough.

We had falsely believed that the dorms were our sanctuary. Not in our wildest dreams did we think that our government would come into the dormitories to assault its youth. We were gravely mistaken.

That night one graduate student, Ezzat Ibrahim Nejad, was shot and killed. Ezzat was the only casualty that was actually acknowledged by name by the government. Why they chose him isn't clear. What I can say about Ezzat, and I only knew him through other friends, was that he was strong and he believed in our movement. I don't believe he was singled out from the rest of us, but I do think the Hezbollah may have seen him resist.

I did see the Ansar-e Hezbollah shoot one student two or three times, and I've often wondered if it was Ezzat that I saw murdered. I was some two hundred feet away, and in the confusion I couldn't be sure of the student's identity. Still, to see a human being murdered in cold blood was a first for me. I couldn't believe what was happening. In my mind, the Islamic regime had sunk to a new low in what they were willing to do to control the people of Iran, and particularly the youth.

The attack went on for around two hours. It seemed much longer, and I can only imagine how every battle in a war must seem like an eternity. When the Basiji had gone, students came out of the dorms and started picking up the pieces of their living quarters. Before long we realized that the number of wounded was very high, so we started making runs to Shariati Hospital. I found several of my friends, and we walked the short distance to the hospital. We arrived before members of Sepah, and hospital authorities told us that there were many more dead than was later reported by the government. We saw broken bones, lacerations, black eyes, and more blood than we could have imagined. We walked the hallways, gathering any information we could about the wounded and the dead. The hospital was like something out of a movie about a war-torn country where the medical facilities can't keep up with all the wounded coming in. There were more injured than there were people to care for them.

What precipitated the attacks on the dorms the night of 18 Tir, or what had been the immediate cause, had to do with the closing of a reformist newspaper called *Salam*, and the protests that took place in reaction to its closing. Earlier that evening we had continued the campaign with another protest inside the dormitories.

To understand the political climate in Iran at that time, it is essential to weigh the costs. I was twenty-seven years old in 1999. My first involvement in politics happened early on when I was a student at Noushahr College. I organized a student protest because of a ruling by the school administration that would invalidate the credits many students had earned over the course of a two-year program. What I learned from that first experience was the power we were capable of when enough of us come together. We marched on the campus and the administration heard us. From that first demonstration I began formulating the cause that would be the foundation of the movement I helped form and have been part of since.

I met Manouchehr Mohammadi in the early days of my academic career. The two of us shared our vision of a government in our country that was democratic and secular. We had grown up with an Islamic government, seen family members fight in the Iran-Iraq War, only to come back to our repressive government. We believed in secular democracy from the legacy left behind by our political history in Iran from the 1950s. Then Prime Minister Mohammed Mossadeqh believed in a government for our country that didn't allow foreign powers to benefit more from the natural resources in Iran than our own citizens. It was for this belief that Mossadeqh fell out of favor with Great Britain and later with the United States. Both governments would later collude to overthrow Iran's democratic prime minister.

Many late night conversations gave birth to what initially was called Students and Freethinkers of Iran, and later was renamed when we joined with two other student groups, the Students' Committee for the Defense of Political Prisoners, and the Iranian Student Organization, which consisted of high school students. We formed the National Union of Iranian Students and Graduates (NUISG).

Ours was a friendship based on a belief in the legacy of our twentieth century political hero and Iran's former prime minister, Mohammed Mossadeqh. In 1953, Iran had a democratic government and a prime minister who believed in freedom for the citizens of Iran. Mossadeqh was overthrown in a coup that was orchestrated by the CIA and Great Britain, but his legacy continues to live on in the hearts and minds of Iranian people.

Manouchehr and I started the National Union of Iranian Students and Graduates and traveled outside of Iran together as emissaries of Iran's new student movement. The year before the dorm attacks, we had been very active in challenging the government of the Islamic Republic of Iran. We took part in many protests within Iran, and made a name for ourselves as part of the student movement that looked to change the government.

I lived every day back then as if it could be my last. My time with family was minimal, as I knew they would worry, and because I wanted to keep the government from suspecting their involvement in my politics. In fact, my family knew very little of the political work I did. The only member of my family that knew of my politics was my youngest brother, Arash.

In the days that followed the attack on our dorms, we were incredulous. We couldn't believe what we had witnessed that night, and in solidarity and anger, we came out each day in greater numbers. Manouchehr and I left the hospital and returned to the dorms to decide how we would react to the attack on so many students. We started organizing members of our group right away.

What seemed unusual, after having spent so much time outside of Iran at this point, was that the news about what had happened that Thursday night wasn't covered by the media on Friday. Very little press coverage occurred on Fridays in 1999, and the government was likely trying to decide what their story would be. It was our jobs to start spreading the word, but this proved to be a challenge for our group.

One issue that was a recurring theme in our group from the start was a lack of funding. This was in part by design, as our core group believed then, as many of us still do today, that taking money in any form would be a mistake and would misconstrue our message. We never intended our movement to be about making a profit. This carried with it the problem of never having much money with which to operate.

The other weakness we had at that point was that we had not yet constructed a communications channel, such as a newspaper, magazine, radio, or TV station, through which to get our messages out. In July 1999 this presented us with additional challenges, as we had to rely on media outside the country to help enlighten the rest of the world.

Manouchehr and I, along with others in our group, started making calls, first to other Iranian universities and dorms, and then to as many international Iranian media outlets as we could. We contacted news agencies in Los Angeles and Washington, D.C. Voice of America covered the story of a student attack in the dorms, but inside Tehran, many people didn't even know what was happening. At one point we set up a blockade in front of the Chamran Highway that ran next to the dormitories. We stopped cars to let citizens driving by know what was going on. We had to rely on the news spreading in a very grassroots way, by word-of-mouth.

After we returned to the dorms from Shariati Hospital, we started putting protests together for the following days. We knew that we had to use students to get the word out, and we also felt we should mobilize outside of the dormitories and into the actual grounds of Tehran University.

At one point on Friday morning, while meeting with students, Faezah Hashemi, the daughter of Iran's former president, Ali Akbar Hashemi Rafsanjani, came to the dorms to find out what had happened. Hashemi was at that time a member of the parliament. Hashemi tended to side with the reformists of that time, and while many believed that the Reformist movement was an improvement to the hardliner conservatives in the regime, our group and the reformist's student group, the Daftar-e-Tahkim-e-Vahdat, were divided on many issues. They were followers of President Mohammed Khatami. I believed the attack on students in the dorm was systemic in nature, and since the attackers were sanctioned by the regime, I was angered by any move by reformists from the government who might use the attack as a political platform for their cause.

I looked at Hashemi and started a dialogue to students that was intended for her without speaking to her directly. "Shame on the government of Iran," I began, and went on to criticize all those in the government, conservatives and reformists alike, who could attack the students while they slept. My speech ended by saying to her directly that all those in the government had blood on their hands and were as guilty as if they had personally taken the lives of the students lost that night. Faezeh Hashemi left the dorms without approaching me directly, and we didn't hear from her again.

After that we started moving toward the entrance to the dorm. Our group began growing in numbers as we chanted slogans against the government, against terror and dictatorship. We marched closer and saw that the reformist student organization was also there at the entrance to the dorms. They attempted to change the chants to reflect an opposition only to the conservatives within the government. For example, if we said that "the government had to take responsibility," the reformist students would change the chant to "the conservative parts of the government have take responsibility."

At this point it is necessary to understand the difference between the reformist's student group and our group, The National Union of Iranian Students and Graduates. It was our belief then, and it is still my belief today, that where the reformists in Iran missed the mark was in their support for a continuing Islamic government. The belief in what the United States calls "a separation of church and state" was key to our movement. We believed that religion had no place in the government. The Reformist movement and the likes of President Mohammed Khatami believed in Iran's continuing theocracy. They believed in democracy, but a "religious democracy"—a model that has never existed in history, and one that we would never accept.

Throughout the days that followed the attack on the dormitory, there was a continuing struggle between our group and the reformist students. We started chanting; they tried to change the content of the wording of our slogans. We moved out to the main campus of Tehran; they followed and tried to upstage our speeches. We returned to the dorm areas; they followed and again tried to take the stage. Luckily I had a friend who was part of the reformist student group and he would let me know what their group planned next so we could anticipate their moves. There was a feeling then, and perhaps it has had a lasting impression, that the reformists were a "kinder, gentler" Islamic Republic. For the National Union of Iranian Students and Graduates, this wasn't enough. We sought complete change in government, away from the theocracy that persecuted the innocent and had little or no respect for human rights.

In my mind I believe that had the reformist students not fought the secular students in their protests, we would have had an even better chance in our opposition to the government at that time. The regime was shocked by our resistance, and had we been better able to focus on the real opposition—the Islamic regime—instead of constantly having to respond to the reformist students, we might have done even more than we did. I believe that we would have had a better chance of overthrowing the government and getting more people from within the general population to respond to our struggle if we had not had to focus our attention on the movement of the reformist students.

On that Friday morning, I gave an impromptu speech at the gates to the entrance of the dorms, standing in front of the police. I stood on a table and I began talking about our brothers who had been beaten and killed. I asked students to consider what civilized countries would attack their students while they slept. These were students who sought knowledge. They were students of mathematics and science. These were our future doctors and engineers.

The Ansar-e Hezbollah had never unlocked the girls' dorms following the attacks on the dorms. This was an attempt to keep them from being involved in the protests that were brewing. A group of male students went and broke the locks, freeing the students locked inside the girls' dormitory. At that point a group of female students walked to the front of the line where we protested. There were six or eight of them, and while they wore the mandatory Islamic dress with head scarves covering their hair, they also covered their faces with bandanas to hide their identities. They walked to just in front of where I stood, and they faced the police. There was such courage in their young faces, and there was sadness and anger. I don't know who they were, but I felt great pride at that moment for my brave sisters of Iran.

That day, the Ansar-e Hezbollah were at Friday prayers in the morning, but by noon they were done, and they came out into the streets to engage in counter-protests with the students. They carried batons and bats and had the police on their side as they started antagonizing students from across the entrance line. By four or five that afternoon, our students began defending themselves by throwing rocks and anything else they could find at the Ansar-e Hezbollah.

Some of the students in our group had the idea of making petrol bombs, or Molotov cocktails, to defend themselves. When the Hezbollah became extremely aggressive with us, some of our students made the homemade incendiary bombs that were thrown during the riots. At this point some of the students were arrested by the police and taken to jail.

As students fought back, the police and the Ansar-e Hezbollah started retreating outside of the dormitory area. Before long we had grown in numbers and taken over not only the dormitory areas, but the rest of the Tehran University campus. On Saturday morning, we had planned to protest in front of Tehran University, but the reformist students were already there. We moved outside to Fatami Avenue and protested instead in front of Iran's Interior Ministry. This move proved to be strategic, as it sent a very strong message to the government and to the reformist students. Our group was strong, and we were unafraid. We stayed close to the Interior Ministry for several hours before returning to the Tehran University campus.

The number of protesters continued to grow, and by Sunday night, we had the largest turnout of some fifty thousand students, not just from Tehran University but from other universities in Tehran. Outside of Tehran, the first university to stage protests was Tabriz University. Tabriz is a city in northwest Iran, about three hundred miles from Tehran. Students there heard about the attacks on the dorms and came out to protest, where they were met with extreme violence from the regime. After Tabriz, other universities joined in, including Esfahan, Hamadan, Ahvaz, Mashad, Mazandaran, Gilan, Shiraz, Zanjan, Yasd, Semnan, Oromiah, Hormozgan, and Kerman, to name a few.

In response to our protest, a representative from President Khatami's government, Interior Minister Abdolvahed Mousavi-Lari, tried to give a speech in the dormitories. He began by trying to assure us that all was well, that everything was going to be okay. The students in the audience became so enraged after everything that had happened that they rushed the stage, and in a matter of moments they had removed his head wrap and he quickly left the area.

In support of the students, former Tehran University Chancellor Mohammad Reza Aref resigned from his post as Minister of Communications, but the government ended up not accepting his resignation. In a similar move, reformist Higher Education Minister Mostafa Moin also resigned and was later returned to his post. In truth, our group didn't really accept these shows of support, as we felt as reformists, they were still far too aligned with the Islamic Republic.

On Monday, July 12, 1999, Iran's Supreme Leader, Ali Khamenei, made a television appearance in which he wept as he talked about the student riots. He said that he forgave the students, and while they had attacked Islam, the government would not punish them, but instead invited them to turn themselves in so that a kind of truce or negotiation might be possible. I watched with wonder and a fair amount of amusement, in truth. I asked myself if this man could honestly think that we were so naive as to believe his tears. We all knew that this was the man responsible for ordering the attacks on the dorm.

By Tuesday, the number of students who protested started to dwindle. The regime started sending out troops to control the protesters, and at that point, the arrests of students became the main focus for police. We had finally caught the attention of the global media, and it was a strategic time for our group. Sepah had surrounded Tehran University and the dormitories in a two-mile radius. The leaders of the National Union of Iranian Students and Graduates were at the top of the list of those the police were seeking to arrest. That included Manouchehr, his brother Akbar, Ata Moradi, and me. In the days that followed, we searched for ways to stay free so that we could continue to lead our group. This was the last thing that the Islamic Republic of Iran wanted to see happen.

## THE ANSAR-E HEZBOLLAH

The Ansar-e Hezbollah, literally translated as Followers of the Party of God, are plain-clothed police who carry out unofficial punishment for breaches of the Islamic Sharia law. They officially fall under the Basiji branch of the Sepah Pasdaran. The Sepah, a religious army, also includes Iran's Air Force, Army, Navy, and Quds Force. The Quds Force concerns itself with issues that fall outside the borders of Iran. In recent years, the Quds Force's visibility has come to the forefront during the United State's wars with Afghanistan and Iraq.

Distinguishing between members of Ansar-e Hezbollah from Basiji can be difficult, as some of the religious zealots who are part of this branch of Sepah actually serve in both roles. Many members of Ansar-e Hezbollah are also Basij, and for this reason, in my writing about the attack on the dorms on July 8, 1999, I often use the terms Ansar-e Hezbollah and Basiji interchangeably. They are extremely religious by nature, and they believe they are carrying out the will of the Almighty. Incidentally, the current Islamic regime president, Mahmoud Ahmadinejad, was a member of the Basij in his youth during the Iran-Iraq War. He went on to be part of the Anjoman Eslami Daftar-e Vahdat, which would become the modern day reformist student movement, the

Daftar-e-Tahkim-e-Vahdat. The original group was responsible for the U.S. hostage taking of 1979.

## NATIONAL UNION OF IRANIAN STUDENTS AND GRADUATES

In order to understand how the National Union of Iranian Students and Graduates was constructed, it's important to know who played a part in the leadership of the group. The following biographies are from my own perspective and therefore subjective. The way our leadership played out was largely organic and had grown out of friendships. We did not always agree back then, and today there are still differences in opinion among us. Still, we all agree on one point: in July 1999, students came the closest to overthrowing the Islamic Republic of Iran as any group had before that time.

## MANOUCHEHR MOHAMMADI

When I met Manouchehr in 1995, he was twenty-seven years old. He grew up in the same province as I did, Mazandaran, but he is from the city of Amol. Mazandaran is in the north of Iran, and close to the Caspian Sea. Those of us from that region speak a different dialect from other Iranians, a language referred to as Mazandarani. Manouchehr and I communicated in Mazandarani when we didn't want others to know what we were talking about. He was a close friend, and someone I trusted. Before our trip outside Iran to Europe and the United States, we agreed on more than we did after coming back to Iran.

We were united against the Islamic Republic of Iran, and that made our bond in 1999 very strong.

## AKBAR MOHAMMADI

In 1999, Akbar Mohammadi was twenty-nine years old. He was someone who, when he believed in an idea, would follow it to the ends of the Earth. During the Iran-Iraq war at the young age of thirteen, Akbar was so disturbed by the Iraqi attacks on his country that he tried to enlist in the army. At that time he was denied entry into the war because of his age, but he didn't stop until a year or so later when they finally let him in.

Akbar survived the war and went on to be one of our most active members. Unlike Manouchehr, Akbar wasn't interested in making the decisions. He was our best foot soldier in the student movement. He was there to implement what we decided, and he was extremely loyal.

His strength was what set him apart from most anyone I've ever known. He was fiercely strong against the Islamic regime, and it was that strength that they put to the test in his final days in Evin prison.

## ATA MORADI

Ata Moradi was also from Amol in Mazandaran. My relationship to Ata was built on a strong friendship and trust. He was quiet, but when he spoke we knew he had something important to say. He was a loyal member of our student movement, and his work was foundational to our early success.

Ata survived many difficult days because of his involvement in our group. While we are no longer in touch, I have great respect for the work he did for our group in the past.

## RIHANEH HASHEMI AND FARANAK TAVASOLI

Two members of our group who sacrificed so much and were enormously brave in their work with the National Union of Iranian Students and Graduates in 1999 were Rihaneh and Faranak. Faranak was eighteen years old at the time, and Rihaneh was her mother.

In July 1999, Rihaneh never stopped talking to students, encouraging them to stay strong in their beliefs and never give up. Faranak Tavasoli was very bright and strong in her belief in the work we were doing. Small in stature, she wore glasses and was bookish-looking. She was fluent in English and had a grasp of knowledge about the politics of Iran that was impressive for her age. She had a hope for the future that was charged with energy and optimism.

The work that Rihaneh and Faranak did for our group and the help they gave in the days before we were captured by the government following July 1999 cost them a great deal. Faranak's younger brother, Faramarz, who was only eight years old at the time, ended up being arrested as part of the round up that followed a raid on their house. He was released shortly after, but in the end the death of Rihaneh's husband, a pharmacist in Tehran, held many questions. To this day there is speculation that he was killed by the Secret Police.

Though I am no longer in touch with Rihaneh and Faranak, I'll never forget the work they did for the 1999 student movement.

# CHAPTER 2

# LEADING UP TO JULY 8, 1999

February 2009 marked the thirtieth anniversary of the Islamic Revolution in Iran. While inside Iran the celebrations sponsored by the regime touted the success of the Islamic Republic and the "freedom" it granted to the citizens of Iran, for many of us outside the country, the thirtieth anniversary was a time to take pause and consider the fallout of the events of February 1979.

I was only a boy in 1979, but the events that occurred during the overthrow of the Shah would shape how I was educated and would change all our lives almost overnight. When you ask those who lived through the Revolution what it was like, they often will tell you that one day the country was under the Shah's rule, and the next day we lived under Islamic rule. All bets were off and it was a completely new game.

I am often asked by people who are not from the Middle East how the Islamic regime could have taken power, and how they have stayed in power. The answer isn't a simple one, but one that has many factors involved. The Shah of Iran, Mohammad Reza Pahlavi, had ruled Iran for twenty-five years following the coup that overthrew Prime Minister Mohammad Mossadeqh. In 1979, the Shah's rule was considered a dictatorship. Ayatollah Khomeini had lived in exile for many years, and from Iraq and France he had voiced his extreme defiance against the Shah of Iran. In those early days he never stated that he was going to turn Iran into an Islamic theocracy. He said he was against dictatorship and imperialism, and was very supportive of the poor in Iran.

The other part of the equation was that Khomeini extended a hand of cooperation to other opponents of the Shah. Among them, the communists and other leftist groups, the National Front, and the Mujahadeen all had the common desire to overthrow the monarchy. What they didn't have was a religious infrastructure to ensure that the changes they wanted for the country would stick. What Khomeini could bank on was the institution of the mosque. Then, just as it today, every village throughout the country had a local mosque. As the mullahs blessed Khomeini's campaign throughout the country, this would help later on when the model for a theocracy was presented. Once the Revolution happened, the Islamic clergy fought with the nationalists, the Mujahadeen, and the communists, and later completely turned on them. This is the time when Islamic enthusiasm proved not to be enough to sustain the movement. The ideology alone wasn't reason enough for people to follow the strict rules set by Khomeini, and the Islamic Republic began its march toward violence as a means to control the masses. Thousands of those believed to be in opposition to the government were imprisoned and killed, and what was left was a theocracy that ruled with an iron fist.

In November 1979, with the hostage-taking of fifty-three American diplomats, the Muslim Student Followers of the Imam's Line, who were at that time new and fairly small in number, became visible all over the world. Still, they needed more control of the universities within the country because the secular movement was more powerful and popular among students. The students' secular movement of that time was also better organized. The Muslim Student Followers of the Imam's Line would become what is now the Daftar-e Takim-e Vahdat and part of the Reformist movement of students who supported former Islamic regime President Mohammad Khatami. In 1980, Iran began what the Islamic Republic called The Cultural Revolution—a term borrowed from Mao's People Republic of China. As part of this movement, in April of that year the government closed all universities for what would end up being two years. This was an effort to cleanse the institutions of Western ideology and non-Islamic influences, and part of that cleansing included the expulsion of many students and professors who were believed to be

15

leftist or Western-leaning. Students and lecturers who tried to protest the closures faced imprisonment or worse. The fallout of Iran's Cultural Revolution was that many intellectuals left the country following the closure of the universities.

Upon the reopening of the universities, only students who could prove that they had no affiliation with any "un-Islamic" organization were allowed to return to school. The Dafter-e Takim-e Vahdat grew during this time, establishing offices at universities throughout Iran and growing in numbers. Later, the Basiji also had a presence within universities for the first time. A secular education was all but forgotten, and the universities were taught by members of the regime since they had been purged of any professors who had Western leanings prior to the Revolution.

September 1980 marked the beginning of Iran's war with Iraq and the regime of Saddam Hussein. Although the war that lasted eight long years came with heavy casualties for Iran, with some estimates as high as one million Iranian lives, the war secured Ayatollah Khomeini's position and the new theocracy that he had started. Just as any other country would, when attacked from an outside force, citizens rallied around the ruling government. Those who may not have supported the Islamic Republic prior to the Iran-Iraq War quickly got behind Ayatollah Khomeini after the war began.

As the war continued, and as the casualties became higher, Iranians grew weary of the war with Iraq. The promises broken by the Khomeini regime came to light in time, and the youth in particular, who had been impacted by the new government's rule, started to voice their questions. The exiled Ayatollah who was opposed to dictatorships had come home to create one of the finest.

His promises to have no desire to run the government were the first sign that he had no intention of keeping his word. He put the mullahs in control and they quickly became greedy, creating more corruption in the Iranian government than we had known prior to the Islamic Republic. Khomeini had no tolerance for anyone who disagreed with his mandates. It is estimated that some 180,000 people who disagreed with Khomeini were killed. Khomeini and his cronies were more than happy to take control of Iran, despite all his promises from Paris that he had no desire to do so. Greed, plus an uncanny lack of respect for

Iran's culture or history, became the order of the day under the rule of the Islamic Republic of Iran.

By this time my generation was coming of age, and we sought to understand the true history of our government—not the one that we had been spoon-fed. We saw little chance for our futures because of the double-edged sword of an Islamic government that demanded virtually no freedom of expression and a corruption in that government that allowed the clergy at the top to not only control us, but become rich doing so.

The end of the Iran-Iraq war brought a greater questioning still. The war ended with almost no explanation as to what had happened. We had lost fathers, brothers, neighbors, and friends, and both countries claimed victory in what was ultimately a very costly stalemate. Khomeini said that the war with Iraq was a blessing from God, and for the mullahs, he might have a point. The citizens of Iran who might have opposed Khomeini didn't once the war started. They got behind their homeland. Khomeini used to say, "Jang jang ta piroozi," which literally translates as "War, war, until victory." His almost jubilant support of continuing the war cost the people of Iran greatly. Estimated casualties for our country range from 180,000 to as high as one million.

I was sixteen years old when the war ended. Both of my older brothers fought in the war. If I had learned anything from the years of war, it was patience. I waited and I watched. I waited to grow up, and I read anything I could find that would be closer to the truth from what I learned in school. I watched my worried mother's face as she awaited word about her second son's whereabouts. Not once, but twice, he was reported killed in the war, only to come walking down the long stretch toward my father's farm at the end of the war. I guess in some ways this was life's way of preparing my mother for my own political activity that would prove to bring more than a few grays to her long, dark hair.

I first ran across the name of Mohammad Mossadeqh as a child in middle school. There was brief mention of him in history books, and my brother brought home a book about him on one of his breaks from Tehran University. Thus began my desire to learn more about the prime minister of Iran who was ousted in 1953 by the Shah, with the help of the United States CIA and the British government.

In high school I had one teacher who, when asked, was very open and frank in his answers to me. I began grilling him about Mossadeqh, and as he told me what he knew, he opened my eyes to my own political world.

Mohammad Mossadeqh was from a distinguished family. His mother was a Qajar princess and his father a finance minister in Nasir al-Din Shah's government. Yet, in all his years in public service, having started at the age of sixteen as a tax auditor for his home province of Khorasan, he practiced his own brand of integrity that few before him or since have maintained.

Mossadeqh served in Iran's parliament, the Majlis, and in 1951 was elected as Iran's prime minister. What set him apart was his belief that Iranian citizens should profit from Iran's natural resources. At that time, the British interest in Iran's oil was great, and Mossadeqh was instrumental in taking back control of Iran's most precious natural resource by signing a law that revoked the Anglo-Iranian concession that benefited Great Britain and establishing the national Iranian Oil Company to take its place.

Over the course of the next two years, the British teamed with the United States in what would be the first occasion the CIA overthrew a foreign government. In a project the CIA code named "Operation Ajax" the CIA overthrew the administration of Prime Minister Mohammed Mossadeqh.

In my early research about Mossadeqh, much of the literature available to me from inside Iran was slanted toward the Islamic view. What I read was that had Mossadeqh listened to the Muslim leader of the time, Ayatollah Kashani, his destiny would have been different. In truth, Kashani took bribes from the CIA and assisted with the overthrow.

Much has been written about the 1953 coup in Iran, but not much has been said about what Mossadeqh represents for the youth of Iran today. For many of us, he became a symbol of something so great that we were willing to put our lives at risk to voice our belief in his legacy. By all accounts, he was a passionate man who believed wholly in the idea of democracy. His was a gentle spirit who gave way to bouts of moodiness that could quickly turn to waves of energy that became a force to be reckoned with. He had a great love of country, and was considered overly emotional by some because of the responsibility he took for the poor and disenfranchised in Iran. He was, in essence, the exact prescription current day Western politics would like to see in the Middle East. Yet Western greed plotted his overthrow.

He became my political hero early on because of his approach to secular democracy and nonviolence. He believed so strongly in these ideals that when the likes of Kashani instructed media to call Mossadeqh left-leaning and potentially communist and paid activists came out into the streets chanting anti-Mossadeqh slogans, their activities were not curtailed. In all his years of work in politics, he refused to take pay for his efforts. Politically, he was impeccable with his word and void of corruption.

I believe, as many scholars do today, that one of the events that can be traced to the attacks on the United States on September 11, 2001, is the 1953 overthrow of Mossadeqh. Had Mossadeqh's rule continued, the Middle East would be a very different place today. His overthrow gave way to the Shah of Iran's dictatorship in Iran. While it must be noted that the Shah's rule in retrospect doesn't compare to the kind of dictator rule Iran has known since 1979, the Iranian people were still oppressed during the Pahlavi dynasty.

What the Ayatollah Khomeini and the Islamic Revolution provided for the Middle East was fundamentalist rule. Khomeini inspired the Hezbollah in Lebanon, and Iranian Revolutionary Guards trained them. Khomeini's rise to power signaled the rise of Islamic fundamentalism in the Middle East—a fundamentalism that was extreme in its hatred for Western governments. In essence, the overthrow of Mossadeqh literally opened the door for the kind of extremism that modern-day terrorist ideology is based upon.

In the end, there are scholarly opinions that run the full gambit, from accusing Mossadeqh of error in not being more forceful in his response to the CIA's infiltration of the Iranian government, to a belief that his downfall was his own strongly-held belief in democracy. In truth, had Mossadeqh been able to avoid the overthrow in exchange for forfeiting democracy, I believe he would have chosen to stand by his beliefs to the very end. Instead, he spent three years in an Iranian prison and was on house arrest in his home village of Ahmad Abad for the remainder of his life. Mohammed Mossadeqh died on March 5, 1967.

In 2000, the United States government issued an official apology for the overthrow of Prime Minister Mohammad Mossadeqh. Under the administration of President Bill Clinton, Secretary of State Madeleine Albright delivered the following message:

"In 1953 the United States played a significant role in orchestrating the overthrow of Iran's popular prime minister, Mohammed Mossadeqh. The Eisenhower administration believed its actions were justified for strategic reasons, but the coup was clearly a setback for Iran's political development. And it is easy to see now why many Iranians continue to resent this intervention by America in their internal affairs."

While Clinton's apology was welcomed by many Iranians all over the world, it still falls short in accepting responsibility for the scars that were created by the United States in 1953.

The Islamic Republic used images of Mossadeqh to help sell their revolution in 1979. Yet, they would be the first to persecute those of us who followed his path. The political infrastructure that had been put in place in the early part of the twentieth century was reconstructed with the Islamic Republic's version of the Constitution of Iran. Ayatollah Khomeini used the Constitution to write the laws of the Islamic Republic to suit his own special brand of dictatorship, based on Shia Islam.

As I have said, from his time in exile in Paris, Khomeini's message was that he had no intention of ruling the government of Iran once he returned. According to Khomeini, neither he nor his followers were planning to make Iran into the first successful Shia theocracy in the Middle East. Later, in some of his writing, Khomeini would say that he had made those statements to protect Islam and the future Islamic Republic of Iran.

What Ayatollah Khomeini didn't tell anyone before returning to Iran was the level of cruelty that my country would have to endure at the hands of the fundamentalists who took control. Nowhere was that more apparent than in the 1988 killing of political prisoners, sanctioned by Khomeini himself. Starting on July 19, 1988, a systematic operation began to execute as many political prisoners as the government could. The government was mostly focused on Mujahadeen, as many had been perceived as being against Iran in the Iran-Iraq War, although members of the Communist Tudeh Party and other leftist groups were also targeted.

Thousands of political prisoners were executed in the five months of the secret operation. Many of those killed were awaiting their release, having served their prison terms. While the operation was very secretive, because of the magnitude of the killings, news leaked outside the prison walls.

The systematic interviewing of each prisoner, asking a different set of questions depending on whether or not the prisoner was a Mujahadeen or a leftist, were followed by hangings in sets of six prisoners. In Iran, the method of hanging takes longer than in other countries, as the prisoner is lifted from the ground instead of dropped, taking sometimes as long as fifteen minutes before death occurs. During the five-month operation, executioners had complained of being overworked due to the nature of the hangings, and had requested firing squads instead. To this the Islamic Republic responded that hanging was the preferred method of execution under sharia law when dealing with apostates and enemies of God.

Many of the bodies of the political prisoners executed in the 1988 operation were buried in unmarked mass graves in Khavaran Cemetery—a gravesite normally used for non-Muslims. In recent months there has been much talk from the Islamic Republic about destroying what currently exists at the site. This has spurred public outcry, since so many family members go to the unmarked graves every year to remember their brothers, fathers, sisters, mothers, and children buried there.

What Ayatollah Khomeini designed in the theocracy of the Islamic Republic of Iran is what could be considered a leadership monopoly—the Supreme Leader himself having all branches of government eventually report up to his authority. The way in which the system was designed has proven to insulate first Khomeini and now Khamenei from any threat of loss of power.

The way the model works is ingenious in its way. The *Vali Faghih* or "Supreme Leader" as he is called in English, is essentially the highest "available" authority in Iran. What I mean by the term "available" is that the Supreme Leader is considered a lesser authority than the concept of the Twelfth Imam, the Mehdi, or lesser still to that of the concept of Allah.

The Mehdi is a concept of Iran's unique brand of Shia Islam, which believes in a hidden twelfth Imam that is estimated to have been born in 869 AD. The Mehdi has been hidden by Allah, according to Iran's Shia Islam belief, for more than 1100 years. The belief is that the Mehdi will return to visibility at a later date in order to bring peace and justice to the world. He is second in command to the idea of Allah, who, as one would imagine, is also fairly unavailable for decisions about the passage of laws, leaving the third in command, Iran's Supreme Leader, in charge. As the successor to Allah and the Mehdi, the Supreme Leader pretty much has unlimited power within the government structure.

Below the Supreme Leader are three entities with a lesser degree of authority: the head of the judiciary, the president, and the Majlis, Iran's parliament. The head of the judiciary is appointed by the Supreme Leader, while the president and the Majlis are elected. Both the president and the head of the judiciary have to meet the minimum requirements of being male, practicing Shia Muslims, and approved by another body of government, the Guardian Council. They also must have complete loyalty to the Supreme Leader.

The Guardian Council is the most influential body of government in Iran, and consists of twelve members, six of whom must be clergy appointed by the Supreme Leader, and the remaining six are nominated by the head of the judiciary and approved by the Majlis. The head of the judiciary is chosen by the Supreme Leader—another very nice set up that ensures loyalty to the Supreme Leader.

Another body of government that is designed to provide the appearance of a separation of powers, or a "checks and balances" idea, is the Majlis Khobreghan, or as it's called in English, The Assembly of Experts. The Assembly of Experts is responsible for appointing a new Supreme Leader upon the passing of the current Vali Faghih. Its members in theory are supposed to monitor the performance of the Supreme Leader and should he be deemed incapable of fulfilling his duties, remove him from office. In practice, this has never happened. The Assembly of Experts is made up solely of clerics, and while they are elected, candidates much first be vetted through the Guardian Council. Again, this circles back to complete control of the Vali Faghih since, as we know, is the most influential body of government in Iran and is made up of all the Supreme Leader's cronies.

A body of government that was promised early on but never came to fruition was the Majlis Moassesan, or Constituent Assembly. This body would have consisted of some three hundred representatives and would have eventually dissolved the Assembly of Experts. The Majlis Moassesan was never created, and in fact, when the original amendment was presented to Khomeini, he dismissed it and called it a conspiratorial act. The Majlis Moassesan's absence in the new government was a bone of contention for Abbas Amir-Entezam, who would be imprisoned for pushing for its creation. Amir-Entezam would later become known as the Mandela of Iran, spending some twenty-seven years in and out of Iranian jails.

What is important to note about all these bodies of government is that ultimately, in some form or fashion, they all eventually lead back to the Supreme Leader. The Supreme Leader appoints the Head of the Judiciary and the Guardian Council. The Guardian Council qualifies the president, the Majlis, and the Assembly of Experts. The Assembly of Experts qualifies the Supreme Leader, returning back to where it all began in a nice full circle. Under these conditions, the Supreme Leader is basically guaranteed the job for life.

The Constitution of the Islamic Republic is rife with contradictions and inconsistencies. From an early age, I took an interest in political science, and as my political activities evolved, I spent time studying the Constitution. I knew that one day being able to quote the Constitution could very well come in handy.

The preliminary draft of the Islamic Republic's Constitution was written in Paris in the first half of 1978. A final draft was approved by the Assembly of Experts in November 1979. What follows are a few of the articles of the constitution that were of particular interest to me in my political work. These articles would later surface in my battles with the Islamic Republic's court systems due to my political activities in the student movement.

## ARTICLE 5

"During the time when the 12ᵗʰ Imam (may God expedite his appearance) is in occultation, in the Islamic Republic of Iran, the leadership of the affairs and guidance of the people is the responsibility of a just and pious jurisprudent, aware of the time, courageous, of drive and initiative whom the majority of the people know and accept to be their Leader. In case no such jurisprudent has such a majority, a Leadership Council consisting of jurisprudents meeting the above requirements will assume the same responsibility."

It's no surprise that a theocracy based on the belief in the Twelfth Imam coming out of "occultation" one day and reappearing would have mention of The Mahdi throughout its constitution. What I take exception to in this and many of the articles in the document is that within the space of a paragraph, already we see an "out" for the original intent. As stated in Article 5, the government should have a leader that everyone agrees to, but if that's not possible, then the Leadership Council can give the role to whomever they see fit. The Supreme Leader is not an elected official, so how would people express their approval of him?

## ARTICLE 23

"The investigation of individuals' beliefs is forbidden, and no one may be molested or taken to task simply for holding a certain belief."

Articles 23 through 27 needs very little commentary, as they are almost comical in the sense of how much the Islamic Republic ignores their existence. Still, in the Article 23, it is worth noting that the government in Iran has at times taken a tyrannical approach to persecuting individuals based on only a suspicion of their beliefs, and with no material evidence whatsoever.

## ARTICLE 24

"Publications and the press have freedom of expression except when it is detrimental to the fundamental principles of Islam or the rights of the public. The details of this exception will be specified by law."

Article 24 is fairly subjective. What determines if something is detrimental to the fundamental principles of Islam? The government has the right to interpret whatever they choose to object to in any publication.

## ARTICLE 25

"The inspection of letters and the failure to deliver them, the recording and disclosure of telephone conversations, the disclosure of telegraphic and telex communications, censorship, or the willful failure to transmit them, eavesdropping, and all forms of covert investigation are forbidden, except as provided by law."

Again, the constitution makes a very lofty claim in Article 25, only to nullify it with the last statement "except as provided by law." One might ask the question, why bother writing Article 25 at all?

## ARTICLE 26

"The formation of parties, societies, political or professional associations, as well as religious societies, whether Islamic or pertaining to one of the recognized religious minorities, is permitted provided they do not violate the principles of independence, freedom, national unity, the criteria of Islam, or the basis of the Islamic Republic. No one may be prevented from participating in the aforementioned groups, or be compelled to participate in them."

Article 26 again sounds like a very worthy law up until it states "provided they do not violate the principles of independence, freedom, national unity, the criteria of Islam, or the basis of the Islamic Republic." Almost anything can fall into one of these categories, and land members in an Islamic regime prison before they have their first meeting.

# ARTICLE 27

> "Public gatherings and marches may be freely held, provided arms are not carried and that they are not detrimental to the fundamental principles of Islam."

In truth, Article 27 is just an extension of Article 26. Any Basiji or member of Ansar-e Hezbollah can interpret a public gathering as detrimental to the fundamental principles of Islam anytime they choose.

# ARTICLE 38

> "Any kind of torture used to extract an admission of guilt or to obtain information is forbidden. Compelling people to give evidence, or confess or take an oath is not allowed. Such evidence or confession or oath is null and void. Any person infringing this principle is to be punished in accordance with the law."

Human rights violations in Iran are nothing new, and the Islamic Republic's blatant use of torture is well-known. Amnesty International's 2008 Annual Report for Iran states that torture and ill-treatment of prisoners is widespread throughout the country. In my own political activities, I have argued for Article 38 in front of interrogators who essentially said that torture was supported in Islam if a prisoner is suspected of lying.

Following the 2009 presidential elections and the protests that landed thousands of demonstrators in Islamic regime prisons, one of the leading candidates, Mehdi Karoubi, wrote a letter of concern to Hashemi Rafsanjani, head of the Expediency Council, on July 31, 2009. In his letter, he cited the abuses of political prisoners, including the torture and rape of both boys and girls. He asked Rafsanjani to appoint a committee to look into the abuses. After receiving no response from Rafsanjani, the letter was made public.

The significance of Karoubi's letter as it relates to Article 38 of the Islamic Republic of Iran's Constitution is that it represents the first time that a ruling cleric has brought torture to light in the thirty-year reign of the Islamic Republic.

# ARTICLE 168

"Political and press offenses will be tried openly and in the presence of a jury, in courts of justice. The manner of the selection of the jury, its powers, and the definition of political offenses, will be determined by law in accordance with the Islamic criteria."

Article 168 is another piece of the Islamic Republic's Constitution that I argued while in custody. It is not uncommon for political prisoners to be tried and convicted in secret courtroom sessions at which they may not even be present, much less have representation of an attorney or be heard by a jury. In my last stay in an Islamic regime prison, I endured four months of interrogations, torture, and isolation before I ever spoke to a judge. At that hearing I had no representation and no one was present in the courtroom except the judge and those guarding me.

The extent to which the Supreme Leader of the Islamic Republic has a monopoly on control of the laws combined with the extreme contradiction of terms of the Constitution make for a government that is very difficult to break open. The system has worked for thirty years to ensure that overthrow is avoided, and while some have come close, and inside Iran is a pressure cooker of dissatisfied citizens, still the Islamic Republic is sealed tight.

What makes the government so strong? One of the largest factors besides how the laws have been constructed is the control of wealth by the clergy. Khomeini ensured utmost loyalty when he designed the infrastructure of the government of Iran. He placed clergy in strategic posts throughout the government. He then set up what has been called the "Institutions of Clergy Power."

Khomeini set up institutions that would assure the power of the clergy was secure. These institutions ranged in function from security organizations like the Revolutionary Guard to Organizations for Propaganda and Supervision. They are organizations that report directly to the Supreme Leader and into which even the president of Iran has no visibility. They are not taxed and they make the clergy who work for them enormously rich while the average citizens of Tehran may work two or three jobs just to survive.

The outcome after twenty years was a sense of frustration felt by my generation. We had become weary of accepting the contradictions of our government, and out of those conditions was born a new brand of student movement.

# Chapter 3

# Those Who Left

In the years before July 1999, there were few people whose influence touched me as deeply as did Daroush Forouhar. Every Monday we met at his house. He and his wife, Parvaneh, would serve us tea out of very small and delicate clear tea glasses, and he would talk to us about politics. These were the years that formed much of my political beliefs about the future of Iran.

Forouhar was the founder of the Nation of Iran Party (Hezb-e Mallat-e Iran), started in 1951. The party was founded on the idea of secular democracy and the separation of religion and government in Iran. Although fairly young at the time, Forouhar was a contemporary of my greatest political hero, Prime Minister Mohammad Mossadegh, whose nationalist approach to governing Iran has always been the foundation for my own political ideology. The Nation of Iran Party strongly supported Mossadeqh's democratic government, and Forouhar was close to the prime minister throughout Mossadeqh's brief time in office and during the overthrow of his administration by the CIA and British Intelligence.

Forouhar was an outspoken opponent of the Shah of Iran until the Revolution of 1979. He briefly supported the new government that replaced the Shah's, and was for a short time the Minister of Labor in the Provisional Revolutionary Government in 1979. Later he began a strong campaign against the clerics who had taken over our country. This opposition to theocracy would continue for the rest of his life.

There is a well-known story that I had the opportunity to verify with Forouhar about when Mossadeqh was invited to the wedding of Dariush Forouhar to Parvaneh Eskandari in 1952. Mossadeqh was unable to attend, but said to his friend Forouhar that Parvaneh was a perfect match. This was a kind of blessing given by the prime minister, and he couldn't have been more correct. Mrs. Forouhar was sensitive, strong, and kind. She was her husband's closest ally and confidante, and she never stopped working tirelessly at his side. She was a political force in her own right, and I believe, had she lived, she would have been a strong leader in our country today.

I first met the Forouhars in person in 1995. I had of course heard of them long before that, and Manouchehr had actually met them before I did. Forouhar, and I call him by his last name only out of affection and familiarity as well as respect, knew of our work as well. He welcomed our ideas and became a kind of role model for me during that time.

The house in which they lived in Tehran was modest. In the living room, among family photos of their two children, Arash and Parastou, were three distinct portraits, one of Mossadeqh, and two others of nineteenth century Iranian constitutionalists and national heroes: Sattar Khan and Bagher Khan. These portraits spoke to Forouhar and Parvaneh's lifelong commitment to Iran and a government in which democratic rule for their country outweighed any idea of monarchy or theocracy.

One of the first impressions I had when visiting their home was that they were true intellectuals. The presence of books in their house, of their own writing and that of others they respected, was just one way this was apparent. But more than that, the way in which they spoke to us, and to each other, was very thoughtful and thought-provoking.

During those meetings, Forouhar took me under his wing. He spoke very slowly, considering every word to ensure clarity. He had a kind face, smiling as he spoke behind his trademark thick Persian mustache. He wore clothes that were more common in the '50s, official but distinct, as if they were from another time. In truth, everything about Forouhar seemed from another time, like he was born to exist a hundred years before and he was on loan to us in the twentieth century. He was a focused listener, paying attention to every word that we said, and digesting it before he responded. He was also very outspoken in his criticism of the Islamic Republic—something that very few people had the courage to do in the 1990s.

First and foremost, Forouhar loved Iran. He had a vision of starting a new united Iran that was of the kind that had existed during Mossadeqh's time, but that could have been better suited for a more modern Iran and a global world that would finally understand the value of secular democracy in Iran. When he spoke, he was careful to use Persian words as much as possible, avoiding words that had been adopted from Arabic as part of our language. He was a purist this way, and unlike anyone I had ever met.

He encouraged me to continue with our student group, and he thought I should eventually leave Iran and work abroad as the representative of the student movement. When our group suggested sending me outside of Iran, Forouhar thought Germany or Austria would be the best part of the world for me to continue my political activity. I started to learn German, and it was Forouhar's suggestions that were in large part the basis for our planning a trip outside of Iran to visit Europe and the United States.

Manouchehr and I started planning our trip in the summer of 1998. My family was very much opposed to me leaving Iran, first out of fear that I might not return, and second out of fear for what might happen to me if I did. Because of their concerns, I asked Manouchehr to go to Turkey first without me, and in a few days, once my family relaxed into the knowledge that I hadn't gone, I would join him.

Before I left for Turkey, I went to see Forouhar one last time. He sat with me and proceeded to prepare me for what to expect. It was my first time leaving my country, and there were so many new things to experience. I had an idea what to expect from the trip, but Forouhar provided me with ideas that I hadn't entertained before talking to him.

For me, I was curious about Iranians outside of Iran. We were from a generation that hadn't known Iran before the Revolution. I was just a child when the clerics took over, and my only knowledge of Iranians was the people I knew in my country. I also wanted to know about all the other groups that were organizing outside of Iran. We had been contacted by several of them that had heard of our protests, and we wanted to know what their thoughts were and how we might join with them in our political work within the country. The last reason for me was that I had never been to a Western country. I had seen movies—mostly Westerns with the voices of John Wayne and other actors dubbed with Farsi. The Islamic Republic was comfortable with its citizens watching American Western movies since there was very little interaction between men and women, and what little that existed was very proper and not sexual by any means.

Forouhar warned me about the reception I might have from Iranians outside of the country. He told me, "Don't expect them to applaud you when you get off the plane." He went on to say that their first question would be, "If you are truly against the government in Iran, why did they let you leave?" He went on to remind me that this would be when I had to remember our goal, and that I would understand how much more work we had to do. As he always did, he warned me to be very cautious wherever I was, inside or outside of Iran, because the government of Iran had far-reaching arms that could make murder seem like an accident. It was his way of saying, "Look both ways before you cross the street." He knew this from having lost too many friends who thought they were safe after they left Iran.

Another thing that Forouhar told me that I'll never forget, and that I have in fact adopted as my own from time to time, is that his wish not that he die an old man in his bed. Whatever way he left the earth, his wish was that it be in the process of doing something for the good of his country and in support of his goals. His political work was what gave him satisfaction. I believe it was the same for Parvaneh.

That visit would be the last time I saw Forouhar. On November 22, 1998, Forouhar and his wife Parvaneh were brutally murdered in their home. Forouhar was stabbed eleven times, and Parvaneh twenty-four times. I believe they both knew this was a likely end to their lives, but that makes it no less tragic. Neither of them were afraid to die for their beliefs, but I can't help wondering what more they might have done for Iran had they lived into their nineties. At the time of their deaths Forouhar was seventy years old and Parvaneh was sixty.

I got the call from Manouchehr when I was in Turkey. He had gone on to the United States by that time. I could tell by the way his voice trembled that he had been crying. He told me of the murders, and we were both shocked and saddened by the news. We debated going back to

Iran for the funerals, but we both felt Forouhar would have encouraged us to go on with our plans. With a very heavy heart, I left Turkey and went on to Germany to meet with Iranian groups there.

I heard that more than one hundred thousand people came out into the streets to remember Forouhar and Parvaneh. Young and old alike felt the loss of these great leaders of the secular movement of Iran.

When calling home, we got mixed messages about the situation. On one hand, people were so sad about what they knew was part of the government's plan to kill those who questioned them. We felt we should be there, but the message was clear from inside and outside of Iran that we should stay outside of Iran. In truth, we had already become problems for Iran. Our leaving the country was the catalyst for a kind of change, and the Islamic Republic was in a quandary. If we stayed outside of Iran and sought political asylum in Germany or the United States, the government could say, "See, they always wanted to leave." They could launch a campaign against us and the overall opinion of us might have easily been that we were part of the regime since the government had let us leave in the first place. If we returned to Iran, while it was obvious we would be in grave danger, it would be difficult for the Islamic Republic to label us as spies since we had returned.

Of those who complicated matters further, President Khatami's reformist students were at the top of the list. While the conservative media in Iran was already reporting inaccurately that we had applied for political asylum in Germany, the Daftar-e Tahkim-e-Vahdat reformist students called us "suspicious" for having left Iran, insinuating that we were connected, after all, to the conservative government. The reformist students had media and financial support. They had offices at all of the major universities, and they had power.

I stayed in Meintz for that month. I met with several Iranian groups in Germany. My impression of Iranians outside of Iran was mixed. It's difficult to comprehend how people can change culturally once they leave their homeland.

My generation was the first to live in the Islamic Republic of Iran. We were fed its ideology in schools, taught often by its party members. But what the new government in Iran never accounted for in 1979 was the growth of technology that the next thirty years would yield, or the hunger with which its younger generations would seek to know what was happening outside our country. Satellite technology and radio were both windows outside of Iran. Even after satellites were banned, we still found ways to hide them within our homes so we could see how the world outside was changing.

Nearly three quarters of Iran's population is under the age of thirty-five. With the birth of the Internet, the Web brought pop culture into Iran, and today young Persians in the larger cities are as image conscious as their contemporaries in Los Angeles, Tokyo, or Paris. What the Internet brought to the youth of Iran was the picture of what freedom looked like. They saw youths outside their country moving through their societies with the freedom to question rules—even those imposed by their governments. While the streets of Tehran were draped in the chador worn by women and the separation of boys and girls who were not familial, behind closed doors the youth became as Western as those in London or New York.

The cultural divide in Iranians was fairly obvious in Europe, but most apparent when I went to the United States. The first American city I visited was Austin, Texas. Manouchehr met me there. We had been invited to Austin by Mohammad Hasibi. Hasibi was a supporter of the National Front of Iran, founded by Mohammad Mossadeqh in the late 1940s. He supported us financially while we were there. Next we went to Dallas, where we met with Nasser Mehman, a monarchist who had been sent to the United States by the Shah of Iran to learn about submarines and never left. In Dallas we were asked to give speeches at a meeting of the Iranian Cultural Association.

What we realized early on was that overall, people who had been outside of Iran for any length of time had very little understanding of what was really going on inside Iran. They came from a country that no longer existed. Convincing them that they might need further education on their own country was an undertaking we weren't interested in pursuing. They didn't understand what the new generation in Iran was facing. They had a memory of what they had left, and it was very different from our reality. We became saddened by what we saw, and in all honesty, I wanted to return home as soon as possible. Still, we had many new things to learn in the United States and Europe, so we remained outside Iran for close to six months.

There were a number of groups that we encountered outside of Iran—all of them with memberships made up exclusively of people whose origin was Iranian, but diverse in their approaches. One thing they all shared in common was a curiosity about our group and the two student leaders who had come out of Iran to meet with them. At that time, what we did was unheard of, and there were times when even we were astonished that we had made it that far out of the country. We had no idea what waited for us back home once we tried to return.

What follows is a brief description of the groups we met outside of Iran, including details about how we were received by each.

## IRANIAN MONARCHISTS

Monarchies are nothing new to the culture, but in 1925, the most recent of them began with the Pahlavi Dynasty. Led by Reza Shah until he was deposed in 1941, the role of king was given to his young son, Mohammad Reza Shah, until the Revolution of 1979 caused him to seek refuge in the United States until his death in 1980. The twentieth century Pahlavi Dynasty was a constitutional dynasty, meaning the monarch worked in tandem with a prime pinister and a Majlis, or parliament.

Although strictly outlawed inside the country, present day Monarchists of Iran are very common outside of Iran in Europe and the United States. Many of the Monarchists who left Iran after the fall of the Shah came with money to begin their new lives in the United States and other Western countries.

In general, Monarchists outside the country are suspicious of any movement evolving inside Iran. But the main group of Monarchists who invited us to Europe and the United States were mostly supportive of our movement at that time, even though our ideology was different from theirs.

## MUJAHIDEEN-E KHALQ ORGANIZATION (MKO)

There is often confusion when the media covers terrorist activities and refers to jihadists as mujahideen. While the term is correct, it doesn't specifically refer to the Iranian group Mujahideen-e Khalq Organization (MKO). MKO was started in 1963 by a group of students, and at their founding they were in extreme opposition to the government of the

Shah of Iran. They participated in the Iranian Revolution of 1979, but have since become one of its strongest opponents.

MKO's ideology is said to be a mix of Marxism, nationalism, and Islamism. They have been based at the Iran-Iraq border since 1986, but there is currently a lot of discussion about them losing this as a base due to the U.S. occupation of Iraq. During the Iran-Iraq War, the MKO lost a lot of support inside and outside of Iran because they lived in Iraq. The new generation is suspicious of MKO because of its Islamic base. There are also many Iranians who cannot forgive the MKO for being in Iraq during the Iran-Iraq War, and many believe the MKO was aligned with Saddam Hussain.

In 1998, the MKO was not in agreement with our group's ideology because of our secular foundation—even though they have at times claimed support for separation of religion and government. They also didn't agree with our nonviolent policy. Still, they didn't attack us and were for the most part supportive of our visit. I met two people in Texas who were introduced to me as members of MKO and tried to interrupt our speeches. I later found out while in prison that they were actually members of the Islamic Republic Secret Service. I mention this as a side note only to demonstrate again the far-reaching arms of the Islamic Republic.

In truth, the MKO has lost more members at the hands of the Islamic Republic of Iran than any other group.

## NATIONAL FRONT

Mohammad Mossadeqh's National Front still exists today, and they were perhaps the most supportive of all the groups we visited outside of Iran. Ten years later, their numbers are far less than before and they are geographically divided.

## LEFTIST GROUPS/SOCIALISTS

There are several groups that would be considered "left" or communist or social democrats. We encountered several of them on our trip. Many of these groups have great ideas, but there is a lack of cohesive structure among the groups overall, and for this reason, plus the fact that there may or may not be actual leaders of these groups, they are difficult to actually call by name. Some leftists supported us, and some did not.

One group, the Worker-Communist Party of Iran (WPI), has a strong presence in Europe, but they also have members in the United States. This group was one of the first to express concern about Manouchehr and I visiting Europe and the United States WPI published a paper during our visit that accused us of being sent from the Islamic Republic and working for the government. In all fairness, it is not uncommon to have a certain level of suspicion when it comes to dealing with the Islamic Republic. When so many people have been killed in the name of that theocratic government, it is only natural that a sort of paranoia develop outside of the country. We understood their concerns; however, it didn't lead to much dialogue with this group.

Later, when we were imprisoned, this group changed their stance about us.

Manouchehr visited several other places in the United States, including California and Washington D.C., but I only visited Texas on that first trip. We had been asked to come to Sweden, England, and France, but because of our financial situation, we returned to Germany where we had backing to send us home. We were both anxious to return to Iran—as much from being homesick as wanting to take back what we had learned abroad and start working on our next moves.

Upon returning to Germany, the search for who had been involved in the murders of the Forouhars was heating up in the international community. We would later hear that the deaths of the Forouhars were part of a larger scheme to silence those of us who challenged the Islamic Republic. There were many others who were killed or disappeared in what became known as the Chain Murders of Iran. A list of people marked for execution eventually surfaced, and coincidentally it was carried by an Iranian secret service agent named Majid Bagharian, who was in Germany at the same time Manouchehr and I returned there after our visit to the United States Bagharian was caught, and as fate would have it, my name as well as Manouchehr's was on that list, which included some fifty-three people.

German police knew we were in the country and contacted us through the friend with whom we stayed in Meintz, Mehdi Jaferi Gorzini. They warned that we were in extreme danger at that point and assigned a bodyguard to us for the next month. We were both still very saddened by the deaths of Forouhar and Parvaneh, and staying inside the apartment where we were essentially under house arrest for our own safety added to a feeling of wanting to return home. Then we heard of the next killings, writers this time, Mohammad Jafar Pouyandeh, Majid Sharif, Firouz Davani, and Mohammad Mokhtari, from the Bagharian list. This was little more than a couple of weeks after the Forouhars had been killed, and it reinforced to me that this was part of a much larger plan, and that we had no choice but to ride out this time in Germany.

We were offered asylum by the German government, and as tempting as it was, we declined on the basis that we felt a responsibility to go back to Iran to fight for the change we believed could occur. The odds were against us, and we really didn't know what we would find when we returned. There had been conservative newspapers articles published inside Iran warning us not to return. When we called Iran we couldn't get an accurate picture because at that point any number we called was being controlled by the Iranian secret police.

Before we returned, we made contact with students in our group and they organized a sit-in at the airport to greet us upon arrival in Tehran. They had some one thousand students ready to come out, but the secret police paid Manouchehr's brother Akbar a visit before we returned. They told Akbar that if there was a demonstration at the airport, we would pay a heavy price and so would our family members, who would be imprisoned as well. This was too high a price to pay and we decided not to let the students come to the airport.

Manouchehr and I decided that we should not both return at the same time, that one of us should stay in Germany awaiting word that it was safe to come home. Manouchehr volunteered to return to Iran ahead of me. We devised a code for how we would know it was safe for me to return. When Manouchehr called me, if he said the name of President Khatami three times at the beginning of our conversation, I would know all was safe to return. If he called me and told me all was well, but didn't mention Khatami, I would know not to return.

At that time, all the Iranian media outside of Iran was on standby awaiting word on us. Had the Islamic Republic jailed us immediately upon our return, the press would have been overwhelming in the global community. The Islamic Republic must have known this and intentionally avoided it. The day after Manouchehr returned to Iran, I caught a flight home.

A nonstop flight from Frankfurt to Tehran takes just over five hours. I cannot say that these were the calmest hours I've ever spent in my life. Returning to a violent regime that was not particularly happy to welcome me back into the country held its share of concerns. I wasn't at all sure that I wouldn't be hauled off to jail within minutes of landing.

At the same time, what we had learned from our trip outside the country had left me charged with so much emotion that just deciding what we had to tackle first became a challenge. There was a part of me that was disappointed at what I'd experienced in Europe and the United States. Our vision for the future had completely changed. We had a kind of paradigm shift in the making, and we mourned the naive way we had looked at Iranians outside the country before our trip. Before we left Iran, we had heard of all the groups who were operating outside Iran, and we believed that if we could just make contact with them, that from within the country we could be the catalyst that would bring about change. These people we had heard of were giants in our minds.

Upon traveling among all the different groups outside Iran, we came face to face with the reality that the groups we so looked up to were all fighting among themselves. Now, I won't say that there in-fighting didn't exist among political groups within the country. As I mentioned, our student movement had regular run-ins with the reformist students, for example. But outside the country, these Iranians had freedom. That was the difference between us. We thought that given that freedom, they would have all been working together, but it wasn't so.

The other thing that bothered us was the lack of Iranian youth involved in political groups outside the country. Most of the people who were involved had been out of the country for twenty years or more. They didn't have a grasp of how Iran had changed since the Revolution. They made decisions based on a memory of what the government was in 1979 or some other time. At that time the Internet was just becoming popular, so there wasn't the widespread media that exists today.

What we brought back to the Islamic regime was the knowledge that we had our work cut out for us. We were energized, but what we believed before we left, that change would happen quickly with all of us working together, was going to take some re-thinking. We knew that we had to bring all the groups together—monarchists, republicans, and socialists alike—to support the new generation inside Iran. The Mujahideen-e Khalq were too far underground in Iran to even make contact at that point. Our only requirement would be that they believed in a secular government and that the means to change the government would happen in as nonviolent of a campaign as possible.

I can remember the pilot saying we were in Iranian airspace, and at that time I had a feeling of excitement and happiness to be back inside Iran. Even knowing the uncertain outcome of my return, to be back home made it all worthwhile. I didn't know it then, but that would be the last time I would fly into Iranian airspace for quite sometime. As of the writing of this text, I have yet to be able to return.

When I landed in Iran, it was without incident. My family was there to greet me, and I went home with them to recover from my long trip.

My family home is in the province of Mazandaran along the Caspian Sea. I grew up in the city of Babol, and my family is an old one in that region. My father raised five children as a farmer, growing rice and citrus trees. My mother took care of both sets of grandparents and four boys and a girl. I am the middle child in my family.

When I returned, the worry on my mother's face was tangible. She had aged during my six months away. During my visit to Babol, my father and the rest of my family spent hours each night trying to dissuade me from continuing in my political work for Iran. They were afraid of what would happen to me, and they feared for what the government might do to them as well. The only one who looked at me with complete respect and loyalty was my youngest brother, Arash.

Arash was sixteen years old at the time. I was eleven when he was born, and I had taken my role as his mentor very seriously from the day of his birth on. From a very early age, I could see how bright Arash was. He excelled in school and was able to form conclusions out of very complex ideas. His devotion to me was so strong that nothing could have ever changed his feelings. He listened to me talk about what I had experienced, what I believed was possible for the future, and I could see in his young face that he was hooked. He was as passionate about his love of Iran as I was, and he would fight to change the regime there with every bit as much dedication as I.

While my oldest brother tried to discourage me from continuing, my father watched me and my reactions. I believe that other than Arash, my father knew me best, and he knew I had made up my mind.

One afternoon he asked me to take a walk. We went outside to the rice fields that make up so much of the land that my father has lovingly fed, manicured, and grown over most of his life. Rice grows like long blades of grass, and in Mazandaran, when the gentle wind blows in from the Caspian Sea, the rice plants do a dance to the coaxing of the wind that is truly spectacular. I remember thinking that afternoon as I walked with my father how much I loved it there in my home. In my travels outside Iran I had seen many impressive, beautiful sights, but none could compare to this.

My father asked me if I had made up my mind. I said I had. He told me that he respected my cause and what I was trying to do. He went on to tell me that as my father, he couldn't stand thinking of what could happen to me if I continued.

He told me a story about Mossadeqh's time that he had never told me before. "One thing you don't understand, Reza Jan, is how politics in Iran can change very quickly. You weren't there to see the way it was when they overthrew Mossadeqh. One day, everyone loved him. They were out in the streets chanting 'Long live Mossadeqh.' But when it was all said and done, those same supporters might be out in the streets on the very same day, holding pictures of the Shah and chanting 'Long live the Shah.'" I told my father that it hadn't been the same people, and he went on to explain that what he meant was that the names and faces might change, but in the end it was all part of the politics of Iran.

I told him that I understood, but that I believed this time it would be different. Our numbers were greater, and our supporters were strong in what they believed. I had chosen to take this fight to the end. I reminded him that he had four other children, that there were many in our country who only had one child, and when they lost that child because of the injustice of the Islamic Republic's system, they had no more children left. I told him that if he only lost one of his five children for the sake of Iran, perhaps it was worth it. He didn't comment, but his silence told me that he knew he had lost this battle. He would respect my choice despite what he really wanted.

When I left Mazandaran to return to Tehran, I wasn't sure when I would see my family again. My mother cried when I hugged her goodbye. My sister did also. Arash looked into my eyes in that way that he has. Now, at twenty-seven years old, his face has grown into that look, but at sixteen his eyes were too old for his childish face. He was my student, my soldier, and my confidante, and he would wait for me to tell him how he could get involved.

My father stood apart from the others and waited. I tried to joke with him, and he smiled a little, but in his eyes I saw his seriousness. He knew then that I was embarking on a future that would be risky and might lead to my demise. Still, he looked me straight in the eye and pulled me to him, kissing each side of my face before letting me go.

# CHAPTER 4

# SETTING THE WHEELS IN MOTION

If I were to try to capture the essence of the student protests that followed in the months after our return to Iran, it would be nothing were it not for the music that was a backdrop to our movement. Three songs in particular capture the passion of the students in our group, and the love we all felt for our country. We sang them at every protest, and along with the chants for freedom that were spoken at each gathering, they became part of our unity.

The first song, "Ey Iran," is not the official national anthem of Iran, but for many people it represents the true sentiment of national pride for our country. In most recorded versions, it begins with a baritone male chorus and the opening line, "Ey Iran, ey marz-e por-gohar" literally translates as "Oh Iran, oh bejeweled land." Often I have thought when we sing those words that the students of our movement are the jewels of Iran. This is never truer than when I recall the singing of "Ey Iran" at the beginning of all of our protests.

If "Ey Iran" is the anthem for Iranian pride, the second song we sang, "Yare Dabastani Man," is the anthem for the student movement in Iran. Written by Mansour Tehrani in 1980, the title means "My Classmates," and while Tehrani may have written the song in a different time from ours, we took "Yare Dabastani Man" as ours in the student movement of the 1990s and it has continued today as a symbol of student unity. Among the most powerful of the words of that song are:

43

Engraved are the names of you and me
On the blackboard
The scars of the lashes of tyranny
Have stayed on our bodies

The last lines of the song speak to the unity of the students in our group: "My hands and your hands have to tear down this curtain. Who other than me and you will find the cure to this illness?"

In recent years, student members of the Basiji in the Islamic Republic have tried to use "Yare Dabastani Man" in their propaganda, but for those of us who lived through the movement of the '90s, and for those within Iran who are still fighting for justice and democracy, this song is our own.

The third song we sang, "Azadi," was about freedom. It is charged with the longing for a taste of that which is the opposite of oppression. We sang "Azadi" as we locked arms, often to resist the Ansar-e Hezbollah when they opposed us at demonstrations, which was almost always.

It was upon my return from Europe at our very first gathering at the gravesite of Daroush Forouhar and Parvaneh Eskandari Forouhar that we sang those three songs together again. There must have been at least five hundred students who joined us at the place where the Forouhar's are buried in Behesht Zahra cemetery in Tehran. Both Manouchehr and I spoke at their graves, and vowed to Forouhar and Parvaneh and that we would never stop fighting for the goal they had been so instrumental in helping to form. The students lined up and one by one, walked by to touch the graves and make their own somber promises to continue the work for freedom.

The months that followed were full of political activity for our group. We believed our best approach was to insert ourselves into events, anniversaries, and key strategic days of remembrance that would signify our commitment and make a point about our organization.

## 29 Esfand

March 20, or as it is known on the Persian calendar, *29 Esfand*, commemorates the day in which the Anglo-Iranian Oil Company was nationalized in 1951. This is a particularly important day for Iranian nationalists because of what it represents. The date in 1951 marked a shift in how Iran interacted with the West, Great Britain in particular. It was also Mohammad Mossadeqh's involvement in helping to pass the legislature within the Iranian Parliament of that time, the Majlis, to vote on the nationalization of Iran's most valuable natural resource. From 29 Esfand in 1951, the government went on to elect Mohammad Mossadeqh as Prime Minister of Iran.

On 29 Esfand in 1999, our group organized a small demonstration to take place at the ancestral village of Mossadeqh, Ahmad Abad. We were planning a larger gathering in Ahmad Abad later in May to mark Mossadeqh's birthday—May 4 on the Gregarian Calendar, and 14 Ordibehesht on the Persian Calendar.

## 14 ORDIBEHESHT

The basis for our protest on Mossadeqh's birthday would be the freeing of political prisoners in Iran—more specifically, the longest held political prisoner of the Islamic Republic of Iran, Abbas Amir-Entezam. Amir-Entezam was sentenced to life in prison in 1981, accused of having been a spy for the United States. He had a brief release in 1998, but was re-arrested shortly after that, as is common with the Islamic Republic. Our group protested his new arrest.

Ahmad Abad is about forty miles west of Tehran. Mossadeqh's house is where for more than a decade he lived under house arrest following being tried as a traitor in December 1953. The village holds Mossadeqh's memory very dear, and there are custodians of his property who guard its relative ease of existence. Basically, the less activity that occurs there, the more the Islamic Republic is likely to overlook Ahmad Abad. While its custodians protect Mossadeqh's memory, they are careful to also guard the tranquility that exists there. For this reason, the custodians as well as members of the National Front were concerned when our group wanted to come to Ahmad Abad for a demonstration.

In the days leading up to 14 Ordibehesht, we realized that we would need buses to take students from Tehran to Ahmad Abad. As usual, finding funds for such things proved to be a challenge. At that time I had a job in Tehran, working for the water company, but every check went to our group. We had a small office in Tehran, and any activity we planned cost money.

We went to members of the National Front to request assistance, and they agreed to provide financial backing for buses to take students from our group to Mossadeqh's ancestral village. Unfortunately, there were still more students who wanted to go than we have busses to transport them.

Upon hearing that the National Union of Iranian Students and Graduates would be participating in 14 Ordibehesht in Ahmad Abad, the conservative media in Tehran came out in full force. There were about four newspapers backed by the Ansar-e Hezbollah, who came out against us in the news. While each of the newspapers had their own agendas, traditionally they could easily unite on important issues— particularly issues that were strongly opposed by Iran's Supreme Leader, Ali Khamenei. The Ansar-e Hezbollah threatened that if our group came to Ahmad Abad, they would be there waiting for us. The conservatives in Iran have a disdain for secularism and the legacy of Mohammad Mossadeqh that is as raw of an open wound as if he had been prime minister yesterday.

Our group had been forewarned, but we were no less sure that we should go to Ahmad Abad. We took several buses from Tehran to the gates of the village. From there it's about a half mile to the entrance to Mossadeqh's house. Our students carried three large photos. One was of course of Mossadeqh, one was of Forouhar, and the last was of Abbas Amir-Entezam. Almost immediately we saw the Ansar-e Hezbollah. There were also members of the National Front and others who were the custodians of Mossadeqh's property, and they came out to warn us that if we were coming any further, we shouldn't chant slogans or sing political songs that might incite the wrath of the Hezbollah.

We started singing "Ey Iran" as we entered the cemetery where Mohammad Mossadeqh is buried. There were close one thousand students, and we began locking arms, stomping our feet to the rhythm of the words of the unofficial national anthem of Iran. There was great energy among the students that day. We were unstoppable, and this infuriated the members of Ansar-e Hezbollah.

Without warning, they came at us with full force. They began to attack students with batons and bats as they chanted Islamic slogans at us, invoking the name of Khamenei with every violent thrust of their weapons. We did not back down, and there was great strength in our numbers. We were empowered and stood against them. Finally, the Hezbollah arrested two female students and four male students, whom they took to a waiting car.

We became louder after that, challenging the Hezbollah to release the students. I went to the microphone to speak, but because the custodians of Ahmad Abad were worried at how quickly the scene was escalating, they didn't give me the microphone. I began shouting anyway, and told members of Ansar-e Hezbollah that we wouldn't leave Ahmad Abad until they released the students.

From their reaction, this may have been the first time we had ever presented the Ansar-e Hezbollah with an ultimatum. They were shocked at our strength and at the audacity of our threat. At the same time, they knew we were serious and that the scene could easily get more out of hand than it already was. If it escalated at that point, on that day, it would mean not just a student group coming out against the government, but all those in Iran who celebrate 29 Esfand, 14 Ordibehesht, those who still support Mossadeqh and human rights would follow.

Begrudgingly, they released the six prisoners to us, but afterward they called Tehran to ask for reinforcements. Because of the roads, the forty miles that Ahmad Abad sits from Tehran can take as much as two hours to drive. Tehran sent riot police to put an end to our demonstration, but before they had time to arrive, we began packing up to leave. As we headed for the entrance, we were again attacked, this time by members of Ansar-e Hezbollah who wore brass knuckles. They struck me and Manouchehr first because we were at the front of the crowd and obviously leaders. I was knocked unconscious and the back of my head was bleeding from falling to the ground. I had been hit in the face and the ribs.

Before starting the drive back to Tehran, we went to the buses to find all the windshields had been busted out by the Hezbollah thugs. On the road back to Tehran, we saw the riot police pass us from the opposite direction on their way to Ahmad Abad. Manouchehr and I caught a ride with a member of Forouhar's group, who took us into Tehran to Shariati hospital.

At the hospital there was a female doctor who attended to our wounds. While we were there, the hospital received a call from the

Ansar-e Hezbollah. They had been calling all the local hospitals to see where we were. The doctor was kind enough to warn us that we had to leave immediately, that the Hezbollah was on the way. A nurse showed us through a back entrance and when I turned to thank her before walking out the door, I saw that she was crying. She must have had the thought, and it wouldn't have been far from the truth, that it was just a matter of time until the Islamic Republic caught up with us.

We were running on such adrenaline that I don't think we ever stopped to feel afraid. We immediately headed to our small office. Members of our group were waiting there for us. There was a feeling of relief, but more than that, we were invigorated. We celebrated what was in our minds a very significant win. Never before had we been so strong, and the Hezbollah had backed down because of our strength.

14 Ordibehesht would become the first in a series of demonstrations that would both make us stronger and push the Islamic Republic that much closer to a breaking point. Eventually, they would have enough of it, and we knew this. But we also believed that as our strength grew, we were that much closer to changing the government in Iran.

## 2 KHORDAD

In 1997, Mohammad Khatami won the presidency in Iran. This was an important win in Iran for many reasons, but mostly because Khatami was proposing a government that was less run by conservative ideology and more open to democracy. Khatami promised a change from the hardliner conservative approach that has been the order of the day for the Islamic Republic's government since the 1979 Revolution.

To understand the Reformist movement, it is important to look at the dynamic of the culture of post-1979 Iran. The Revolution was made up of many of the young people from our parents' generation. It consisted not only of a religious fervor that put women in chadors and grew beards on our young men, but at the time of the Revolution there were other groups who believed in removing the Shah. Members of the left, for example, joined forces with the mullahs, in complete agreement that the Shah should be overthrown.

Once the mullahs came to power, however, most of those groups were considered anti-Islamic and the result was that the clerics took over. The younger generations of Iran watched as all of this unfolded, and out of that time many of us became suspicious of support from the mullahs of any kind.

With a present day population that is made up of so many young people, Khatami's arrival on the political scene was for some a welcomed change. From our perspective, we felt that the popularity of Khatami was similar to what the United States Democratic Party faced in finding candidates to run against George W. Bush in 2004. In some ways, it was enough that the candidate *wasn't* George W. Bush. But in the larger picture, that model wouldn't prove to be enough, and the Americans would have to wait another four years for a popular candidate to run.

This was how we saw Khatami. The right-wing government of the Supreme Leader of Iran, Ali Khamenei, had left young people so frustrated that anyone *other than* Khamenei was appealing. In truth, the general student population didn't give their support for Khatami's campaign until just twenty days before the election in 1997. It wasn't out of great love for Mohammad Khatami that he was elected, but instead because he gave the people an option for something else. This was our group's stance as the reformist's celebrated Khatami's second year in office on May 22, 1999, or according to the Persian calendar, *2 Khordad*.

That year the reformists announced a celebration for *2 Khordad* in Tehran's Laleh Park. Laleh Park is to Tehran what Central Park is to New York City. Parks in Iran are important, as they provide a meeting place where families as well as young people can congregate outside the home. While unmarried men and women cannot mix freely in the parks, they still offer a way in which the youth can socialize, and as is human, males and females always find a way to each other, even in the Islamic Republic.

When our group heard about the celebration at Park Laleh, we started organizing our members so we had a presence there. What is important to understand is that functioning as a proper group in Iran at that time was extremely difficult. First of all, in order to have any sort of public demonstration, it is required that you obtain a permit from the government. No event sponsored by our organization would be given a permit because since we were secular, we were considered "anti Islam." To deal with this, we often watched for other demonstrations by the reformist students and we would insert ourselves into these activities.

The other area that made putting our organization together very challenging was that we had to rely on making flyers to get the word out. At that time, e-mail wasn't as common as it is today, and even now, logging on to the Internet from within Iran can have its challenges. We relied heavily on flyers and word of mouth communications, so the next hurdle was always where to print flyers. Unlike the United States, where you can walk into a Kinkos and print out a thousand copies, in Iran at that time printing flyers for our group would raise eyebrows immediately. Using printers at the university was risky, so we would have to print fifty here and another hundred there, asking members to sneak into work offices or any other place where they might know of a printer. Nonetheless, we found ways to print flyers and members would give them out on campus and in other locations where students hung out.

The other way we promoted our activities was via radio. Voice of America would give us a plug on events, and so would Los Angeles Iranian stations, which might get heard from within Iran on occasion. There were a few stations inside of Iran that would announce our events, but usually they took great care to not identify how they knew of an event. For example, they might say that they heard about an event from the Internet, when in truth one of our members would have called them. Other Western countries occasionally would support us, but interestingly, the BBC refused to support the secular student movement in Iran.

Not all students who believed in our cause were able to come to demonstrations. They risked being expelled from school in some cases, and for students who came from poor families, the road to getting into a university was too long and difficult to take a chance on losing their opportunity to get an education. Manouchehr and I knew about this firsthand, as we had been expelled from our universities because of our political activity. Also, since the Reformist movement was sanctioned by the government, even though it was in opposition to the conservatives within the country, students who participated in the Reformist movement had futures in the Islamic regime government as much as members of the conservative groups did. Students who took part in our group had little hope for a future in the Islamic regime government.

On the day of the celebration at Park Laleh, our group came in quietly. The gathering that day was largely about the reformists and their opposition, the Basiji and Ansar-e Hezbollah. Each group came holding large posters of their respective leaders—the reformists with photos of Khatami, and the Basiji with photos of Khamenei. We took our place among the crowd, positioning ourselves in the audience to the right of the huge stage that had been set up for the event. One of the keynote speakers from the reformist group was Ebrahim Asgharzadeh. Asgharzadeh's history dates back to his days at Tehran University, where he was one of the leaders of the student group that took over the United States embassy in 1979. By the time Khatami was elected, Asgharzadeh had become part of the Reformist movement.

There were thousands of people in the audience, and from the crowd it was difficult to distinguish who belonged to which group. That was, until we gave a signal to our group, who raised the large photo of Mossedegh as we began singing the unofficial Iranian national anthem, "Ey Iran." Our voices rang out loud and strong and we stomped our feet in rhythm to the song. This was precisely at the time that Ebrahim Asgharzadeh was speaking. At first he tried to speak over our singing, but after the crowds joined in, he stopped his speech. The crowd, drawn to the photo of Mossadeqh, shifted their focus from the stage, and literally turned toward our group. They sang with us, and cheered as we finished the song and moved on to "Yare Dabastani Man." After singing, we chanted slogans in support of the political prisoners being held in Islamic regime prisons. Our chants were about freedom and democracy, and the crowds joined in as though we had staged their participation as part of planning the whole event.

The Ansar-e Hezbollah responded violently. They began using batons and screaming pro-Khamenei slogans as they herded students toward riot police, who began arresting demonstrators.

The day after 2 Khordad, the reformists came out in the press, referring to our group as anarchists.

## 4 KHORDAD

Just two days later we had what had become an annual meeting of our group and Tabarzadi's group. Together we had formed an alliance called the United Students' Front that supported political prisoners who were still being held in Islamic Republic jails. The first year we met in Park Laleh, but the next two years we decided to meet at Tehran University. Our goal at these meetings was to bring students out to show our support and send the message to those still being held for political reasons that we stood with them, and we would not forget them.

Just as we had remembered him during the demonstration at Ahmad Abad on Mossadeqh's birthday, Abbas Amir-Entezam was again foremost in our thoughts. For this reason, we had invited his wife, Elaheh Amir-Entezam, to come to our meeting and to say a few words about her husband.

When we arrived at Tehran University, the first thing we saw was that the Daftar-e-Tahkim-e-Vahdat reformist students had chosen the exact same place and time to have a demonstration of their own for Mohsen Kadivar. Kadivar is a cleric who had been imprisoned by the Islamic Republic on charges of helping enemies of the Islamic Republic.

There were some two hundred reformist students demonstrating at Tehran University. The Ansar-Hezbollah was also there, and when the reformist students started to speak, they were stopped by members of Hezbollah. Frustrated and defeated, the reformist students started to file out of the common area where we all met.

Between our group and Tabarzadi's, there were close to nine hundred students who came out for 4 Khordad on our side. Though our numbers were far greater that the reformists, the Ansar-e Hezbollah was even more adamant that we would not speak at the podium—so much so that they began destroying the microphones and tearing the wires from the devices so we wouldn't have a chance to speak.

I looked among the crowd and didn't see Manouchehr. This was strange, as he was supposed to be at the demonstration, and the two of us usually stayed fairly close during a demonstration of this size. I asked his brother, Akbar Mohammadi, where he was, and he hadn't heard from him. I also checked with Ata Moradi, and no one knew where Manouchehr was.

The crowds started to get restless, and it was beginning to look as though the Ansar-e Hezbollah might succeed in sabotaging our demonstration. Akbar Mohammadi nudged me on the shoulder and said in a low voice that we had to do something quickly or all would be lost. At that point he hoisted me on his shoulders, prompting me to begin speaking. Another student joined him in supporting me, and months later I would learn that the other shoulders I had rested on that day were those of Ahmad Batebi, whose iconic image would later make the cover of *The Economist* magazine as a symbol of the student movement in Iran.

From their shoulders, I began a speech that went something like this: "I welcome you to this day of remembrance, the remembrance of our brothers and sisters who are held by the government of the Islamic Republic of Iran. I welcome you, oh children of Cyrus. I remind you that you are not strangers here. This is your home, and you have every right to stand in this very spot to remember the political prisoners who are held against their will, tortured and robbed of their most basic human rights. You are the children of Iran, and you must show those who oppose you that you will stand strong, that you are here for your brothers and sisters who are held as political prisoners. Those who hold them captive are nothing more than Taliban. They should be ashamed to call themselves Iranians."

At these words, the students began to chant slogans of freedom. I went on, "Brothers and sisters of Iran, children of Cyrus, lock arms and make yourselves a human chain that cannot be broken. Stand up and raise your voices so that those who are imprisoned can hear our cries for their freedom. My leader is Mohammad Mossadeqh, not the mullahs who have no respect for human rights." The students moved together and locked arms. Someone in the crown yelled "Ey Iran," and the crowd responded by starting to sing it and "Yare Dabastani Man."

By this time, we had thoroughly angered the members of Ansar-e Hezbollah. One of them came at me with a knife, and had Akbar and others not pulled my body back quick enough, I would have been stabbed. I was moved to another area and lifted back to the shoulders of Akbar, who before he lifted me had said in my ear that we should start chanting "Down with Akhond." Akhond is the name for clerics, and though I was certainly opposed to them, I didn't think the timing was right to come out with such a strong chant, and I told Akbar that we would save that slogan for a later date. I mention this to demonstrate Akbar's courage. He believed so strongly in what we did that he had no fear. For that and many other things, I hold him very dear in my heart.

From Akbar's shoulders, I introduced our special guest, Abbas Amir-Entezam's wife, Elaheh. Mrs. Amir-Entezam had been standing in the crowd among the other demonstrators, and no one knew who she was until she started to speak. She started by thanking our group and Tabarzadi's group for forming the United Students' Front. She reminded the students of her husband's innocence, and she talked about the death of the Forouhars, expressing the sad loss their murders represented for our country.

After she spoke, I continued to lead students in chanting slogans against dictatorship, and the number of students continued to grow. By that time, there were some five thousand students participating in the demonstration, all at varying degrees of chanting and singing in support of 4 Khordad. The emotions were very high, and I felt that I had connected with the hearts and minds of all those who could hear me as I spoke. I felt my words brought them out even stronger, and for this connection I was high from the adrenaline that day created.

Other students in our group started noticing the members of Ansar-e Hezbollah honing in on me. They warned me that I needed to get out of the crowds as soon as possible. Just then the riot police arrived and began spraying tear gas into the crowd. Even through that, students seemed to face the police unafraid. Several of our students pulled me aside and told me that the situation had gotten too dangerous for me as they ushered me toward the east side of Tehran University and out of the area where we demonstrated.

Two or three hours later, thirty or forty of us met at the home of one of our supporters. By this time I was frantic for word about Manouchehr. One student had seen him on the campus of Tehran University just before the demonstration began, so our worst fear was that he had been arrested. We started calling anyplace we could think of. At one point we called President Khatami's office, and the response was less-than-interested from the voice over the phone.

Emotions were very high during this time. Akbar and Ata were both there, and we felt we were at a place in our movement unlike any we had experienced before. The students that day had ruined the plans of the Ansar-e Hezbollah. The students had seen for the first time that they were empowered, and the Ansar-e Hezbollah had felt it as well. Now we were at a new level, and that would take the Hezbollah's wrath to a new level as well. This might have felt less daunting had it not been for Manouchehr's disappearance, which had unnerved those of us within the inner circle of our group.

That night we made a pact that no matter what happened, we would continue our fight. Those of us in the room that night pledged our allegiance to the cause, and in renewed strength we began calling media outlets in the United States and France.

We had an interview with Voice of America in which we gave the Islamic Republic an ultimatum. They had forty-eight hours to return Manouchehr and any other members of our group that they had arrested on 4 Khordad. If they did not release them, we would stage the largest demonstration to date on 9 Khordad. The protests would take place not just in Tehran, but in universities all over Iran. We would enlist the support of the international media, and the Islamic Republic would have a full-scale riot on its hands.

Two days later, we had a call from the secret police that they would be releasing Manouchehr and others. They put Manouchehr on the phone to assure us that we could trust what the authorities told us.

At this point, we had already started distributing flyers about the demonstration. Suddenly, after seeing the flyers, Khatami's office became interested in helping us to free Manouchehr. We continued planning the event even though we had heard from Manouchehr, since there was really no way of knowing if the Islamic Republic would keep its word.

We had caused concern with the Islamic Republic by this time, and they were sinking to new levels in their opposition to our activities. In anticipation of the demonstration we were planning, they placed police outside the university days before the event. Next they copied the look and feel of our event flyer, making their own that said it was from our organization, stating that the demonstration had been canceled because Manouchehr was being released.

They did keep their word, and eight hours before the demonstration was to begin, Manouchehr was released. Once he was out of jail, we debated within the group about whether we should go forward with the 9 Khordad demonstration. Our activities had heated up to the point that we knew we were teetering on a fine line between growing our movement and having the government clamp down even more violently than they already had. Finally, we decided that despite the fact that Manouchehr and the others from our group had been freed, we needed to come out to stress the point that he had been taken illegally, and to continue to support those who were still in prison.

On 9 Khordad, we made our way to the campus, attempting to enter from another direction. Already there were hundreds of students who had come out to participate. While entering the campus, we heard motorcycles coming up from behind us. The riders were members of Ansar-e Hezbollah. They seized me and six other students and began stuffing us into a patrol car that sat waiting a few feet away. One of my journalist friends was with me, and while he wasn't a member of our group, he was a supporter of ours who worked for IRNA, which is the Islamic Republic's official news outlet. For him to be arrested with members of our group would be grounds for firing or worse. Fortunately, my journalist friend wore a beard and very much looked like the other religious types who worked for IRNA. As I was being shoved into the patrol car, I shouted at my friend, calling him a Hezbollah. He caught on very quickly and retorted back to me angrily, "Yes, I'm Hezbollah and I'm proud of it!" The officers who had grabbed him let him go and threw the rest of us into the waiting car.

The protest for 9 Khordad went on as planned. I spent four or five days in jail, this time at Sarang Sakhaie jail near Hotel Ferdowsi in Tehran. I estimate the time because in all truth, the days spent in Islamic regime jails tend to be grueling, and timelines can blur as hours can seem like days, and days merge into one another making it difficult to distinguish how much time passes.

This was not my first time in an Islamic regime jail. I had been arrested a couple of years earlier during one of our protests, and at that time I had my first exposure to Mr. Sharafi, who at that time seemed to hold the position of authority over the interrogators within the prison system. I remember Sharafi because he has resurfaced several times during my incarcerations.

They took me to a very small room with a thick metal door. It was the beginning of summer in Tehran, and the temperature inside the room that was to be my cell for the next few days was sweltering. I sat, awaiting what I knew would be a series of interrogations that would likely lead to more beatings than what I had already endured upon being arrested.

When I try to describe the interrogators, I'm always struck at how much they all seem to look alike to me. First of all, members of the Basiji tend to dress in a similar fashion. They wear their shirts buttoned to the very top, so as not to expose any skin below their chins. They wear beards that are kept trimmed. Mr. Sharifi was no different from the majority of them. He was of medium height, had thick eyebrows, and a very intense way of looking into my eyes as he questioned me. He didn't need to raise his voice for me to see his anger when I replied in a way that displeased him.

The first time I came face to face with Mr. Sharifi was in 1997. He said something to me that I never forgot. In a mocking tone, he said, "You think you can change this government? You little students are nothing more than a few squawking little chickens. You were a child when four hundred thousand Mujahideen thought they could overthrow this government. And where are they now? They are nobodies. They live in Iraq and we are here, stronger than ever. You and your other little chickens will never change anything in this country."

When I was taken from my small cell into his office on 9 Khordad, I reminded him of that conversation. I asked, "Mr. Sharafi, what do you think of us little chickens now? Now there are more than just a few little chickens—more like a few thousand now." The anger rose in his face. He began to talk about secularism, how it was a Western idea that was basically an excuse for sexual deviance, mixing male and female students. He went on to talk about the arrests that had been made in a small demonstration right after our 4 Khordad meeting with Tabarzadi's group. The meeting was at Azadi University in Tehran, and while I hadn't attended, there were members of our group there, and a few had been arrested. Mr. Sharifi said that the girl students who had been arrested had been examined by female officers, and none of them had been virgins. In my culture, this is a very insulting and disrespectful thing to say about any female. I was angry at his inference and asked to be taken back to my cell right away. I said that members of our group might not have beards or chadors, but we knew who we were, and I asked him to look into the mirror to see who he saw looking back at him. I reminded him of the Islamic Revolution in 1979 when Ayatollah

Khomeini had said of the Shah's rule that they had chosen a monarchy based on the wishes of an old generation, a generation thirty years before that time, that the new generation of 1979 rejected what the old generation had decided for them. I went on to compare our generation to those young revolutionaries, and said, "Now is the time for our generation to reject what your generation decided for us."

If my words made a difference to him, he didn't show it. His reaction was relatively dismissive. He reminded me that our numbers were very small, and that we were insignificant compared to the power of the Islamic regime, before having me returned to my cell. In my room, his words stayed with me for the rest of that night. I wondered how our government could judge its youth in this way. I felt angry, but I also felt even more determined to fight for freedom as soon as I was released.

I stayed in that room for the next several days. I was told that I needed someone to post bail on my behalf, but since I didn't have family in Tehran, this became yet another challenge. Fortunately, someone from our group contacted one of our supporters, Mr. Mashayehkhi. Mr. Mashayehkhi was an activist during Mohammad Mossadeqh's time in office, and he had taken an interest in our group and in me in particular. He was worried about me being in jail and knew I needed financial support. He put his house up as collateral to bail me out. When he came to pick me up, Mr. Sharifi met me at the top of the stairs before releasing me to Mr. Mashayehkhi. Sharifi said to Mr. Mashayehkhki, "This guy needs to watch his tongue. Everything he says is against the law, and eventually it's going to get him in trouble."

After my release, and after celebrating briefly with members of our group, I again went to see my family in Mazandaran. I spent a few days there before returning to Tehran to continue organizing for demonstrations that would take place that summer. I spent my days by the Caspian Sea thinking about the student movement we were building from Tehran. There were times when I felt that our movement had great hope to make changes in the regime quickly. But at other times the reality of how long of a battle we had in front of us occurred to me. At those times, the images of the struggles of the people of my country were what I hung onto. The people of Iran, especially the faces of the new generations, continually kept me strong in my battle to build our student movement.

My last protest before the attack on the dorms was in front of the United Nations on July 5, 1999. I was arrested in front of the United Nations building in Tehran during a protest in support of long-time friend and activist Heshmat Tabarzadi, who had recently been arrested, as well as other political prisoners being held in Islamic regime jails. The jail stay had been uneventful compared to the other brief stays I had endured due to my political activity. Basically, as soon as I showed up at the U.N. building, the secret service police recognized me and picked me up. Their rationale was that having a protest in front of the U.N. building was more high profile than the protests we had at Tehran University and the surrounding dormitories. Our group believed that our protests at Tehran University were more effective, but that was yet another point the Islamic Republic disagreed with us on.

What the months that led up to the attacks on the dorm meant for our movement was key to what happened later. The student movement in Iran had shaken the foundation of the Islamic Republic so much so that they were threatened by our group. Our organization, the National Union of Iranian Students and Graduates, grew from just a few students at Tehran University in 1994 to more than four thousand official members and supporters by July 1999. We had members and supporters from all over Iran who were rallying, from Shiraz to Tabriz to Mashad. After our office in Tehran was ransacked and closed by the Ansar-e Hezbollah, we had offers to open offices in several other cities.

As I remember those days, often I'm struck at how much power our group had at that time. We came very close during the five days that followed the dorm attacks to overthrowing the regime in Iran. We had offers of support from outside the country, but we preferred to revolt from inside. Whether this was the right decision or not, I can only say that on my part, I believed then as I do today that what set our group apart was that we held to our ideals. We didn't take financial support from those who tried to buy our support for their own agendas, and for this I remain very proud of our movement and the students who worked so hard and sacrificed so much for their love of Iran.

# CHAPTER 5

# THE ARREST

Just as the attack in the dorms on July 8, 1999 was not an isolated event, the movement we built in the years preceding that fateful summer was strategic in the way it was built. And just as we could not have anticipated the severity of the Islamic Republic's reaction, I don't think they believed that the National Union of Iranian Students and Graduates would ever have the power to bring out so many other groups and supporters.

Sunday night, of the fifty thousand who came out to support us, there were many other groups other than ours, including Tabarzadi's group of students. But the members of the National Union of Iranian Students and Graduates were very much triggers in leading the way. We were the only secular student group, and we were gaining support not just from inside Iran, but we had the Iranian media outside the country watching with interest and reporting on the events of 18 Tir. The result was that the streets of Tehran that surrounded Tehran University became riotous. There were photos in which the streets looked like a war zone, with riot police in full protective gear and students throwing stones and carrying injured through the streets.

Of the fifty thousand, most were the youth. They were university and high school students who, though they might not be formally in our group, believed in what we stood for and came out to support us. When we protested through the streets, there were people in the apartments above the streets who cheered us on, but when we asked them to come down to join in the march, most of them didn't. So great was the fear of retribution from the Islamic government that average citizens who wanted freedom were too afraid to come out.

By Sunday evening, the Daftar-e-Tahkim-e-Vahdat reformist students had become increasingly irrelevant. In fact, Khatami's reformists had all but joined forces with the conservatives by that time, and Khatami had even come out in the news calling the student protesters anarchists. At this point, he was nowhere to be found in backing many of the students who had helped to put him in office.

We took that opportunity to say what had been on our minds for several years. At that point, we took Akbar Mohammadi's suggestion to escalate our chants and include "Down with Akhoond" (clergy). This was unheard of at that time. The other activity that was a direct hit to the Islamic Republic was when we tore down photos of Islamic Republic leaders that lined the streets of Tehran. Seeing posters of Khomeini, Khamenei, Khatami, and Rafsanjani was common and still is, in fact. To tear them up in Iran is seen as sacrilegious at best, and at worst leaning toward treasonous.

Because of our activities during the last year and the outrage our members demonstrated, Manouchehr and I became two of the biggest targets of the Islamic regime. We knew by then that our lives were in danger, and so did members of our group.

On Sunday night we had a plan to move the demonstration to the southern part of the city, close to the Tehran Bazaar. This neighborhood is largely blue collar and we felt we would expand the support of our demonstration since the residents of southern Tehran tended to be at the mercy of many of the laws the clerics passed in ways the middle class weren't. We had heard that people there wanted to join our cause. This was a strategic move, as it would include the labor movement along with our student activists. On the way we planned to take over the local radio station, Radio Ark.

Within our group we were in disagreement about whether to go to Tehran Bazaar on Sunday night or on Monday morning. I believed, and still do, that we should have gone that night. It was a mistake to wait because by Monday, the streets of Tehran had been taken over by the Revolutionary Guards. This branch of the authorities is more powerful than both the Ansar-e Hezbollah, who are basically religious thugs, and the Tehran riot police. When the Revolutionary Guards are called in, the situation has gotten serious. By Monday they were out in full force and had decreed a curfew to stop the protests. For this reason, we were unable to make our way to Tehran Bazaar and the citizens south of Tehran.

Manouchehr and I decided to go to the house of Rihaneh Hashemi so that we could rest for a couple of hours and decide what to do next. Rihaneh was home with her daughter, Faranak, who was also a member of our group. Rihaneh's eight-year-old son, Faramarz, was also there. They lived on the top floor of a four story apartment building, and another one of our members rented a first floor apartment in the same building. One of our members had given us a cell phone so we could stay in touch with the other members who had gone back to the dorms. It was that very cell phone that we had used to broadcast the sounds of the protests to radio stations outside Iran during the last several days.

When we got to the Hashemi's building, we felt we could relax for a little while. Our members wanted us back on campus, but it had been several days since we had slept through the night, and we needed to regroup. Instead of going to the fourth floor apartment, we went to our member's first floor apartment.

While I was being interviewed by Nasrin Basiri, who worked for both Radio Multi Culti in Berlin and Keyhan newspaper in London, Manouchehr was on the phone with another media outlet outside the country. Just as I hung up the phone, I heard what sounded like twenty or thirty voices yelling in unison "Allahu Akbar, Khamanei rahbar, margbar zedvalayat fagheh." This was the battle cry meant specifically for us, and literally translated means "God is great, down with those who oppose the Supreme Leader."

How they knew where to find us is uncertain, though years later we believe we discovered who may have snitched on us. We had a member who we later found out had infiltrated our group and was actually a member of the secret service. Just a few hours before the authorities raided the Hashemi's house, we got a call from this member asking if we wanted a gun for protection. We refused, and had we taken him up on his offer and been holding a weapon when caught, there would have been grounds to kill us right away. We believe he was the person who gave the authorities Rihaneh Hashemi's address.

What he didn't know, and what the Revolutionary Guards who came to the building didn't know, was that we would be in the first floor apartment instead of the fourth floor apartment. They searched for us in Hashemi's apartment, and arrested not only Rihaneh and Faranak, but also eight-year-old Faramarz. Before his own arrest, our member showed us out to the back of the building and we started an escape that truly was like something out of an action movie.

They say that in desperate times people are capable of superhuman strength, and while I wouldn't say that Manouchehr and I were necessarily superhuman, we definitely climbed walls and jumped between buildings that we would never have even attempted given normal circumstances.

The area where the Hashemi's building is located has many similar apartment buildings clustered together within the block. Each building is a different height and is separated by walls that enclose it. When we walked outside, right away a woman wearing a chador saw us and started screaming, "Here they are!" so that the Revolutionary Guards would hear her. They looked down from the fourth floor of the Hashemi's building and saw us. We began jumping over the walls and heading into other buildings, working through a maze that we hoped would keep us from being caught. In the distance we heard shots from the Revolutionary Guard's guns, something that told us how desperate they were to apprehend us, literally, dead or alive.

From the roof of one building we jumped onto another and began making our way down to a lower floor. We were planning to separate so that, in case either of us was caught, one might have the chance to get away. Another woman came out into the hallway of her apartment and started screaming at us to leave the building. She said that her daughter had missed her college entrance exam because of the student protests, and she didn't want any trouble for her family. Manouchehr and I tried to calm her down, and just then her older son came out of the apartment with his friend. He told his mother to be quiet, that didn't she know that what we did was for them, for the good of our country.

Her son was probably in his late twenties or early thirties, and his friend was likely an older neighbor. Somewhere in all the confusion we had lost the cell phone we had been carrying. The son let us borrow his, and we made one last call to the Los Angeles radio station Sedaye Iran.

Manouchehr's message to the outside world was urgent and ominous. He said that we were in extreme danger, and that it was likely that we would be killed. His call was broadcast repeatedly over the next few months on various news outlets outside of Iran. Once we returned the cell phone to the son, we lost all contact with the students in the dormitory. Shortly after that the Islamic Republic jammed all cell towers so mobile service was disabled.

The son and his friend took us to the basement of the building where they told us we would be safe. We were grateful, but at the same time concerned, since we didn't know them and there was always the possibility that they could turn us in. Still, at that point, we had no other option except to trust that their intentions were good. In a few hours they came to check on us and brought us a change of clothes. Manouchehr in particular needed something to change into, as he had left the Hashemi's house wearing lounging pajamas since we had intended to rest there.

Although we could have stayed there in the basement, we were concerned that the Revolutionary Guards would come back to search the neighborhood, so we started looking at other options. We also had no idea how much information they had on us, and this added to our anxiety. I had wanted for us to go to the mountains of Mazandaran Province and hide out there until the situation cooled down. There are mountainous villages there where I knew we would be safe, and since we spoke the language, we would find help there as well. Manouchehr didn't agree with me on this point. He had left his address book with his brother Akbar, and for this reason he didn't want to leave the city until he had gotten it back. This became a hurdle that we had to jump if I was ever going to convince him to leave Tehran.

Once we left the basement of the building, we used a payphone and called one of my friends who lived in the Narmak area of Tehran. He told us to come to his place right away, and using car services that were on the streets of Tehran, we made our way there. Once at his house, we were able to think more clearly.

I made a call to my youngest brother, Arash, at that point. Arash knew of what was going on, and he was my only point of contact within my family. He was seventeen at the time, but as I have said, he was mature for his age. I had given him a signal in the event that something like this were to happen, and when I made contact with him he knew to go to a friend's house in Mazandaran, as it wasn't safe to talk on my family's phone. We instructed Arash to call Hossein Mohri of Sedaye Iran radio in Los Angeles and tell him our situation. We also had him call Majid Rooshanzadeh, who was the student president of Freie Universität in Germany. Hossein Mohri was able to make arrangements for us to go to either the Swiss Embassy or the United Nations building in Tehran where authorities would be waiting for us and grant us asylum right away.

For the next few days we stayed at my friend's house in Narmak, but his girlfriend lived only a few apartments away, and she was uncomfortable with us being there. Finally, she gave him the ultimatum that if he didn't make us leave, she was going to call the police and have us arrested. Not wanting to cause trouble for my friend, we left.

At that time, Manouchehr and I started to feel the weight of our situation. We understood that because of the danger we were in, we had very few people we could truly count on. We were on the run, and we were alone. We made a promise to one another that no matter what, we were in this together until the end, and that we would stay together. This proved challenging for me, as Manouchehr and I had very different ideas about what we should do next. My suggestion was that we find our way north to Mazandaran and stay in a village in the mountains like Bandpai, which is remote and secluded, but it was not an option in Manouchehr's mind. He thought we should stay in Tehran where we could be close to people in our group.

As I said earlier, the issue of Manouchehr's address book was a big concern for him. He felt without the contacts in that book, he was not going to be able to leave Tehran. As we took a taxi back to the area around the university, we saw that there were helicopters circling the dormitories and Revolutionary Guards everywhere.

Months before July 1999, I had rented an apartment in Tehran that was in the Maydan Golha Square area. I had rented it from one of my friends' family, and since it had been fairly casual, there was no record of my name being associated with the apartment. Manouchehr and I decided to spend Wednesday night there until we could agree upon our next steps. Fortunately, the apartment was still intact, meaning it hadn't been ransacked by the authorities, and we felt safe that only Manouchehr and I knew about it at that point.

The next day, Manouchehr insisted that we go back to the student dormitories where Akbar and Ata still were staying, so that Manouchehr could get his address book. The authorities hadn't yet arrested Akbar and Ata, thinking that Manouchehr and I would likely try to meet up with them, and in this they were correct. Even they wouldn't have thought, however, that we would have the nerve to go back to the dorms of Tehran University.

When we entered the dorms, the campus security saw us right away and called the Revolutionary Guards to come arrest us. We rushed to the second floor, where we knew Akbar and Ata would be. Akbar was furious when he saw us, asking what we were thinking coming to the university. Manouchehr got his address book and assured Akbar that we were leaving immediately, which we did.

We raced outside the dorm, beating the arrival of the Revolutionary Guards. Manouchehr's next idea was that we go to the home of a friend of his family who worked for the parliament. This friend lived very close to the Majlis offices, which was also close to the dorms. I argued that this was too risky, but he believed that it was so obvious that no one would think we would make such a daring move.

One aspect of Manouchehr's personality was that, while he was a good leader in many areas, in my experience he sometimes misdiagnosed human behavior. This was particularly true at the moment we left the university. We caught a taxi and halfway to the home of the family friend I had a sinking feeling. I saw a car behind our taxi that seemed to be following us, and I sensed that they were government agents. My hope was that we wouldn't be recognized, as both our beards had grown out and we wore our shirts buttoned up like religious types.

We arrived at the building where his friend lived. It was attached to the parliament offices, and had security at the front desk. Manouchehr went in front of me and gave bogus names for both of us when he asked for his friend. We were recognized immediately.

This time the government agency that we interfaced with was the worst so far, the secret service, or as they are called in Iran, the VAVAK. During the time before the Revolution of 1979, the notorious secret police organization that was tied to the CIA was the SAVAK. Known for their cruelty and torture, they were disbanded after the Revolution, but the Islamic Republic created their own very similar organization with almost exactly the same mission and perhaps even worse torture tactics and called this group VAVAK.

Building security called members of VAVAK, who were very close and arrested us immediately. We were taken to the basement of the building, which was dark and dungeon-like, and it seemed as though we had saved the agents from having to find a proper torture chamber by coming straight to this building. The VAVAK began cursing us, and though Manouchehr attempted to speak rationally to them, this only seemed to enrage them more. Members of this group take their duties very seriously, even personally. They began taking turns beating me and Manouchehr. These were not interrogators and they cared very little about anything we had to say. Mostly, they had an opportunity to exercise their violent natures, and they were relishing the moment, beating us until we were both bloody and broken, as they yelled at us repeatedly that we were dead men already.

After a half hour or so, they took us upstairs and outside where an SUV was waiting to take us away. I heard one of the agents making a call in which he told the person on the other end to "tell the boss that we have arrested them." To this day I don't know who "the boss" was, but it's clear our arrests were important to someone higher up. From the backseat I saw our photographs taped to the dash of the SUV. The agents all must have had these pictures, and it's a wonder we hadn't been caught earlier as we took taxis around Tehran.

We were blindfolded so we couldn't see where they were taking us. My body felt broken and I was bleeding. They had punched me in the face and broken some of my teeth and my nose. Manouchehr and I were silent as they drove us. We didn't know where we would be taken, but we figured we would likely be killed soon enough, based on our treatment so far.

When we got to our destination, we were taken out and Manouchehr and I were separated. We later found out that we were in one of the darkest places that has ever existed in Iran, Tohid prison. The prison existed in the days of the Shah and at that time was called Bazdashtfhw Committee Moshtarak Zed Kharab Kari. The Islamic Republic of Iran's Supreme Leader, Ali Khamenei, was imprisoned there for just three days during the Shah's rule, and described it as the scariest place he had ever encountered. In 1999, Tohid prison was reserved for political prisoners. Its location was secret, and until its closure in 2000, not many ever knew exactly where it was located. Many of Iran's writers, journalists, and other intellectuals spent months and years there, and over the years, many died there. In Tehran's main correctional institution, Evin prison, prisoners were warned if they didn't cooperate that they would end up in Tohid, a punishment considered worse than death. Tohid prison is now a museum. It's notoriety is marketed as having been the product of the Shah of Iran's time, which it was, but the Islamic Republic's use of it was every bit as brutal, maybe even more so, than when it was used before the Revolution.

Upon our arrival, they told us that they had taken the opportunity after our visit to the university to arrest Akbar and Ata. There were many more of our members there as well—not just from Tehran, but from as far away as Shiraz and Mashad.

To show how important we had become to the regime, we were met at Tohid by the head of the Revolutionary Court, Hojatoleslam Gholamhossein Rahbarpour. He told me that they had been planning to arrest us for some time, but that now was the time that the Islamic Republic was going to finally put an end to my political activities. As he left the room, he quoted the eighth Sura of the Quran saying in Arabic, "Va ghatelohom hatta la takoona fetnaton. Va yakoonaddino kolloho lellah." This part of the Quran means, in essence, "Kill those who conspire as there is no belief except the belief in Allah." Rahbarpour then turned to the guards on his way out and said, "Interrogate them and then kill them both."

# Chapter 6

# Prison

The days that followed were excruciating. I lost track of time, never knowing if it was daylight outside, or if we were in the middle of a night. The only indication was the call to prayer, but between long interrogation sessions in a torture room and hours in between where I stayed in a tiny room awaiting my next session, time blurred.

That first night was Thursday, July 15, 1999. I remember that first interrogation session in which there were several people in a room firing questions at me and making menacing threats with the objective of scaring me into confessions. I'm not sure how many were in the room at one time since they kept me blindfolded, but I do remember the voice of my principal interrogator, who would become very familiar to me over the next few months. At one point he said, "We were watching you when you gave a speech just a few days ago. I bet you never thought that in less than a week you would be here with us." They brought up my trip outside of Iran, accusing me of treason, and letting me know that many people had been killed for far less serious crimes than mine.

My expectation was that I would die that night. I had little doubt that they planned to execute me, and though I knew I would endure torture that would make the idea of an execution seem like a welcome end to the pain, I also carried a very large burden. Both Manouchehr and I held certain knowledge that could not only be used against one another, but could also cause the arrest, torture, and execution of members of our group and their families. We had the responsibility to our members to protect them. We had to be the veils that would cover their identities, just as the bandanas many of them had worn during our protests had done. But the cost would be great, and I had to keep my mind sharp so as not to slip in telling inconsistent stories.

My belief about how much to tell during an interrogation is that while they continually assure you that if you tell the truth they will stop, they will be your friends, they will help you somehow, they are the real liars. In the accounts of Islamic regime prison torture I have read over the years, often torture victims will say that they had done nothing wrong, and they tried to be as honest as they could, yet they were continually tortured. The truth does little in those situations, and in my case, if I had told the truth, there were many people who would have suffered because of my truth. My experience is that honesty will be used against the torture victims in court, and if it is at all possible to withhold the truth, the odds of saving innocent lives are much higher.

Still, I had to be very careful in when to lie and when to tell the truth. I had learned from previous times in jail that there were ways to tell just enough truth, things that were insignificant but easily proven, so that the real nuggets that the interrogators looked for could be hidden.

The other idea that turned out to be false in my case was the belief that they knew everything about my life, my activities, and everyone around me. In truth, there were many things they didn't know and that I was able to stall them from finding out. For example, they didn't find out about the apartment I had been renting until later. This was of particular concern to me as I had hidden a list of National Union of Iranian Students and Graduates members under a carpet in that apartment. There were close to two thousand names on that list, and had the authorities found it, every one of them would have been in danger. Months later I would find out that my youngest brother, Arash, went to the apartment to find the list. Though they had ransacked the inside of my place, they never found the list under the carpet. Arash took the list and destroyed it while I was in prison.

In the interrogation rooms I was forced to write long declarations about my activities prior to being arrested. Often my interrogators made me write the same scenarios over and over again in hope that I would change the details slightly so that the differences in the stories might provide additional information. After each interrogation I was taken into the downstairs torture room. I was blindfolded for most of this, pulled down the stairs and thrown facedown onto a small bed or cot.

The most common torture was foot whipping. They fastened my hands to the head of the bed and tied my ankles to the foot of the bed. Then they began beating the bottoms of my feet with some sort of hose or cord. When I heard about this sort of torture before I experienced it, I couldn't imagine that hitting the bottoms of the feet could cause such pain. In reality there are so many nerve ending in the feet that after the first couple of blows, the pain is no longer centralized in the feet, but goes all over the body. That night there were several torturers in the room, and one of them sat on my back, bouncing with each lashing with the cord to my feet so that there was the added sensation that every vertebrae in my back would break under his weight.

The torture room was intentionally kept dark. It was large, with the bed at one end and at the other end along the top of the wall, a large metal pipe that ran the length of the ceiling and was sturdy enough to hold the weight of a prisoner. This was where they practiced a torture method called Ghapani. The prisoner was forced to put one arm over his shoulder and reach around and grab the other wrist from the waist. The wrists were then secured, either with a rope or handcuffs, and the prisoner was hung from the ceiling by the wrists. The pain was excruciating. There are no words to describe it.

After the first torture session, they took me to what would be my first cell at Tohid prison, room 410. I wasn't allowed to rest very long, and in truth, it's very difficult to relax after a torture session because of the pain, and also because you tend to expect them to call you again at any moment, so your nerves are raw.

It wasn't long until they came back for me. I don't know if it was that same night or early the next day. I was taken back to the interrogation room where they began questioning me again. They asked me if I knew Aidin Khoshbonyani. I mumbled his name, looking as though it didn't ring a bell, and said that I couldn't recall. I said that I had met many people outside the country, and I couldn't remember all their names. Khoshbonyani was one of the organizers of an interview and speech Manouchehr and I had given in Frankfurt, Germany, that had been televised. They continued asking me about him, and I continued to deny knowing him.

Next, they asked me to write out that I didn't know him, and if they were able to prove that I did in fact know him, I would gladly let them execute me. I wrote the words as though I was sure I didn't know Khosbonyani. During my time in prison I wrote what would amount to literally reams of paper with declarations. At the top of each paper there are the preprinted words from the Quran, "Annejato fessedgh," literally translated, "The truth will set you free."

After I wrote that they could kill me if they proved that I knew Khoshbonyani, they took me to another room where they had queued up a taping of the interview and speech in Frankfurt. There we were, on the screen, sitting at a table in a panel-like discussion: me, Manouchehr, and Aidin Khoshbonyani. I felt the hair on the back of my neck stand up, but I sat still in my seat until they grabbed me and took me back downstairs to the torture room. There they told me that they would teach me what would happen when I lied to them, and the torture session was even more brutal than the first.

After that, I felt my only alternative was to kill myself. My reasoning was that in the end I might have a better chance of protecting the information that I knew, and in truth, I was not made of stone. The torture was unbearable. In the first few hours after that second beating, I asked to be taken to the showers so that I could perform the Islamic ablutions or ritual bath before saying my prayers. When we wanted to communicate with the guards, there were papers in our cells that we could slip through a small slit in the door. They quickly responded to my request and took me to the showers.

There I removed the government issued uniform, a shirt and pair of pants made of jersey material, and began fashioning them into a rope with which to hang myself. This wasn't my first choice for how I wanted to die. In fact, the idea of hanging was terrifying, but no more so than months of torture. The guard who was supposed to be watching me stood just on the other side of the wall, so I was careful to work quickly and make as little noise as possible. I threw the end of the makeshift rope over the piping in the shower stall and climbed onto the railing next to the showers, putting the noose over my head. I jumped from the railing, praying that it would be over soon. Once my weight caught and I felt the tightening around my neck, the piping from above bent and I fell to the ground. The guard heard the crash and came running into the stall.

I was taken again to my main interrogator, who was angry that I had attempted to end my life. He said, "You don't have the right to end your life here. Here, we are the ones who decide when it is time for you to die." At that point, I reminded him of my constitutional rights to a court hearing. In Iran's constitution, prisoners must be taken before a judge within forty-eight hours of their arrest. At that, the interrogator balked and said, "Forget about the constitution here. Here, we are your judge and your jury."

This wasn't the first time I brought up Iran's constitution. During my political activities, I had studied the constitution of the Islamic Republic in great detail. While much of the rhetoric there was yet to be approved after twenty years, the foundation for certain constitutional rights was still there. During one of my interrogation sessions, I questioned the use of torture, as it is clearly against Article 38, which states, "All forms of torture for the purpose of extracting confession or acquiring information are forbidden. Compulsion of individuals to testify, confess, or take an oath is not permissible; and any testimony, confession, or oath obtained under duress is devoid of value and credence. Violation of this article is liable to punishment in accordance with the law." They answered that they were acting under the law of the Quran, which gave them the right to torture in the case of a prisoner who knowingly lied.

Thus began the routine that would be my life for the next 137 days. When they beat my feet, they usually gave me fifteen to twenty lashings. Afterward, they would take me outside to a small courtyard within the building. There they would force me to run on my bleeding and battered feet. The reason for this practice is so that the blood flows back to the feet. I believe this causes the healing process to speed up a bit, and in that way they are guaranteed to be able to continue beating the feet in the next session. If the blood didn't return, then the skin would break down quicker and they would have less success in continuing this practice. Whatever the reason, running on feet that have been beaten to that extent was how they tended to end our torture sessions, and it was no relief. After running it felt like there were a thousand needles piercing every square inch of the skin on the soles of my feet.

For some time, I wasn't sure who was left of the other student leaders. The torturers would say things to lead me to believe that they were dead. They would say, "Your friend begged for his life before we killed him," and I would wonder if they had killed Manouchehr or others. What still is incomprehensible to me is that the torturers seemed to really enjoy their jobs. They laughed through much of the sessions. It is a concept that baffles me. How they could spend hours torturing other human beings, and then go home to wives and children, mothers and fathers, and act like they had just another job?

At times they would bring me into one of their torture sessions to make me watch. I believe they took me to watch Manouchehr and Akbar be tortured, though my mind has blocked some of this. Manouchehr later told me they had brought him into my torture sessions and made him watch me be tortured.

For the most part, I was alone between sessions with my interrogators and the torturers. As I have said, the rooms where they kept me were lit twenty-four hours a day. My first few weeks I was in room 410, but later they moved me to another room, which I believe was 136. The latter room had a dirty carpet that covered about four square feet of the four by six foot area. The rest of the space was a dirt floor. I was not allowed to shower, and I wore the same clothes for my entire stay at Tohid. The only way I could sleep in that space was on all fours, burying my head into my forearms to block out the light. Even today, sometimes I wake up from a bad dream, and I am sleeping in that same position.

The days passed, one into the next. Sometimes I would hear others being tortured. To this day, I'm not sure if I was hearing it while it happened of if they put a tape recorder by my door. During those times I would listen to see if I recognized the voice of the person being tortured. My mind would play tricks on me and I would think I heard Arash's voice. The pain of thinking they had my youngest brother was far worse than any torture I would ever endure. Later, when I talked to other people who were tortured, they told me they had similar experiences, and that they had believed they heard the voices of their loved ones.

The interrogations continued, and I was able to withhold information that would hurt others. I told them what they wanted to hear about those who were outside of Iran, because I knew they couldn't harm people in Europe and the United States. They asked me about Mehdi Jafari, with whom I had stayed in Germany, and my hosts in Texas: Mohammad Hasibi, Hasan Masali, and Nasir Mehman.

My days were filled with writing things that they knew already, and I tried to keep my stories as consistent as possible. The idea of dying became a comfort to me. I knew that if they killed me, I had died for my belief, and in that I was satisfied. Still, I never stopped worrying about my family and Arash in particular. They didn't seem to know about his involvement, and I hoped they would never find out.

During those days of being grilled by my interrogator, they started putting a lot of pressure on me to go on state-sponsored television to admit my involvement and to apologize to the Supreme Leader, Ali Khamanei. I had seen people being paraded on Islamic Republic-controlled TV stations before, and knew that once they taped the interviews, the prisoners where executed. I held out for as long as I could, and the interrogations and torture sessions grew more intense because of my refusal.

Finally, I decided that if they intended to kill me anyway, I would go ahead and let them film me. I would try as best I could to be true to my beliefs, so that anyone who knew me and saw the taped interview would be able to read between the lines of my replies.

On the day of the filming, I was given a suit and was able to take the first shower since I had been arrested. My beard had grown quite long, and I was able to shave it off at that time. They took me by car to a special studio where these sorts of videos were filmed. I was, as always, blindfolded and forced to lie on my side in the backseat. However, at moments I would try to raise my head just enough to see outside, and I thought we traveled east of Tehran, though I don't know this for certain. I was told by the guards driving me to keep my head down, and I remained blindfolded until we reached the station and they took me inside the building.

As soon as I walked through the doors, I saw Manouchehr standing in front of a mirror attempting to arrange his hair. I walked up behind him and said, "They're going to kill us and you're worrying about your hair." We were able to smile at the joke, knowing that there likely was truth to it.

The experience of seeing a friend after weeks of torture and solitary confinement is really a very sweet moment. I had been lied to about who was still alive, and with the exception of seeing torture sessions of my friends', I had no way of knowing if they were still alive. That was definitely true that day when I got to see Manouchehr. Like me, he looked tired and weak, but he was alive, and at that moment, that was enough.

Before the interviews began, the crew that worked for the station applied makeup to both our faces to hide the noticeable bruises. This was the first of two days of filming, and during those days we were treated fairly well. That was just one of the surprises I encountered. Another was when I saw the familiar face of a local Tehran anchor, Bijan Nobaveh Vatan, who would be our interviewer. Up to that time I didn't know he worked for the government. Later he went on to become a conservative member of the Islamic Republic Parliament. At one point during our interview session Vatan slapped me, telling me I was wasting his time.

One sticking point of my interview was that the interrogators expected me to apologize to the Supreme Leader for my participation in the National Union of Iranian Students and Graduates. Because I wouldn't do this on the first day, I faced a particularly difficult torture session on the evening of that day. The next day I told my interrogator that I was ready to apologize, but that they would have to allow me to do it my way. With the camera aimed at me I began, "I apologize to the person who represents God and who delivers God's messages, and who has power over the entire world—the highest power on the earth and the sky, Ali Khamanei." The ridiculousness of these words coming from my mouth was enough to show that I had been coerced into saying them, and for this the film editors never were able to use that footage.

On those two days of filming, I was also able to see the face of my main interrogator for the first time. He was probably in his mid to late thirties and one of his eyes seemed to be artificial. Likely he lost it in the Iran-Iraq war. When I looked into his face, he asked me if I thought he would look scary, and I said that I didn't.

I tried to pay as much attention to those around me as I could in the odd chance that I somehow lived to talk about it later. One face that I saw that day was that of Ruhollah Hosseinian, who was the intelligence minister deputy. He had also been implicated in the Forouhar murders. I pretended not to recognize him, and he quickly turned away, but his presence at the filming speaks to how high profile our televised interviews were. He went on to serve in the Iranian Ministry of Intelligence and National Security (or VAVAK) and as a member of the Council for Spreading Mahmoud Ahmadinejad's Thoughts.

When the edited versions of our interviews finally aired, they were shown with the film clips of our speeches in Germany; however, the Islamic Republic said the speeches were made in the United States, as they were a better enemy for the government.

As I have said, the filming was a slight break in the normal rhythm of my time in Tohid, which consisted of daily interrogations and torture sessions and my return to a small cell where I was alone for hours at a time. One time, as a kind of psychological torture, I was given a copy of the latest conservative newspaper, *Kehan*, because there was an article they had published about our group. The newspaper named our group as the main student organization that led protests in July 1999, and went on to say that four of our top leaders had been sentenced to death. Though they didn't name who they were, I could only guess that it would be me, Manouchehr, Akbar, and Ata.

During the long hours of solitary confinement, I thought of friends and family. I played the events that had happened over and over in my head, but I would go on to envision what would happen to all of them once I was killed. Although making any sort of noise was strictly forbidden, at times I sang "Ey Iran" and "Yare Dabastani Man" while I was alone in my cell. Those songs got me through many difficult hours of loneliness and uncertainty.

On only two occasions the guards put other prisoners in the cell with me. Having company at those moments provided unbelievable relief. The first, Mehdi Khakfirouz, was in my cell for two days within the first couple of months of my time in Tohid. He was a journalist I knew of, and he also had heard of me. In the beginning we were both careful of one another, not fully knowing how much we should trust the other. In the end we talked freely. Mehdi didn't believe they would kill me. He told me he had heard through a visitor who had come to see him that the student leaders who were being held there had a lot of public support both inside and outside the country. This was the first I knew of that support.

Before he was taken from my cell, I asked Mehdi if he were released before me to visit my family and assure them that I was okay. He promised that he would, and I later heard that he went to Mazandaran to see them while I was still in jail.

The only other time I had a roommate was one day when they put Hossein Shariari in my cell. Shariari was in his sixties and was part of the Pan Iranist Group. We sang "Ey Iran" together, and I think it helped him as much as it did me to have some human contact. After he was taken from my cell, I felt a deep loneliness and sadness. I wondered what fate he faced, and I wondered about my own. He came from a different generation than I did, but we wanted the same freedom for Iran.

Finally, after more than three months in Tohid prison, I was told that I was going to have the court hearing that the constitution guarantees after forty-eight hours of captivity. I was taken to the Revolutionary Court in downtown Tehran. When I got to court, it was the first time I had seen my family. I later learned that they had made the journey from Mazandaran to Tehran on many occasions during the last few months, but each time they had been turned away until now.

When I walked into the waiting room that leads to the room where my hearing would be, I saw my mother and father, my oldest brother, his four-year-old daughter, and Arash. My niece, Neda, had insisted on coming when she heard that they were going to visit me, and my family had allowed her. I walked up to my mother and reached out to hug her. At first glance she didn't recognize me because my beard had grown long, and I had lost quite a bit of weight. When she saw me she hugged me and began to cry.

I had two guards from Tohid on either side of me, and I was careful not to speak Mazandarani so it didn't seem that I was trying to hide something from them. At the same time, I tried to appear strong and as upbeat as possible for my family. I picked up my little niece and held her for a moment. My oldest brother greeted me with the traditional kiss on both cheeks and another hug in which he said under his breath, "You have an attorney. His name is Bahman Keshavarz. You can't give up. He will take the case, but you have to put it in a written request." I knew of

Mr. Kehhavarz, who was the head of Iran's Bar Association. My brother also asked me if I knew where they were keeping me, and I replied that at that point I still wasn't sure where I was being imprisoned.

I looked into my father's eyes and I saw that he was on the verge of crying. I had only seen that in my strong father one time before, when my grandfather died. He and my mother looked small and sad, and it killed me to see what my time in jail was doing to them. I was particularly relieved to see my youngest brother, Arash. I didn't show him a lot of attention because I didn't want the guards to notice my attachment to him for any reason.

My family had not known what to expect upon seeing me. They knew I would have faced torture, and they were terrified to see what might have been the result. The face that I tried to show them was one of strength. I once again reminded my father that he had five children, and to be strong. If he lost me, he at least had four other children, and he would be losing me for the sake of Iran. I left him with the lines of a poem by Saadi, *"Khoda kashti anja key khahad barad aghar nakhoda jameh bar tan darad."*

At that point, I was called into the room where my first hearing took place. The room was simple, with a table at which the judge sat to hear my plea. Hearing my case was the deputy of the revolution courts who had seen me for previous jail stays. In front of him was a stack of papers that consisted of months worth of my writing from my interrogation sessions, and on a board next to the table was a list of all seven offences for which I was being charged. He looked at me and said, "Welcome again, Mr. Mohajerinejad. I told you before that you were going down a dangerous path, but you didn't listen, and this time is different." To this I replied that I was innocent of all charges. I asked that I be represented by an attorney of my choosing as opposed to a court-appointed attorney. To this the judge asked me who I wanted to represent me. I said I wanted Shirin Ebadi, Mehrangiz Kar, and Bahman Keshavarz. I requested all three, knowing that as high profile as each of them was, I would be lucky if the court approved any one of them. To this he replied that none of them would be suitable for this case.

He began going through each of the charges against me, to which I was able to give an answer to my innocence on each point.

## THE CHARGES AGAINST ME

1. Threat to national security
2. Leading riots into the streets
3. Founding a movement against the Islamic Republic of Iran
4. Leading a movement against the Supreme Leader Ali Khamanei
5. Founding an illegal group, specifically mentioned as the National Union of Iranian Students and Graduates and our involvement in the protests of 4 Khordad, Amad Abad, and Park Laleh
6. Treasonous actions in leaving Iran to meet with leaders of groups that opposed the Islamic Republic of Iran, and meeting with foreign governments that opposed the Islamic Republic of Iran
7. Attempting to overthrow the government of the Islamic Republic of Iran

After going through each of the charges, the judge told me that based on the information he had just from my writing, he had enough evidence to keep me in prison for the rest of my life. I mentioned the dorm attack and the violence of the Ansar-e Hezbollah who had been involved, asking what punishment they would receive. The judge asked me how I knew anything had happened in the dorms and I told him it was because I had been there, and I had witnessed their actions firsthand.

He ended the hearing by telling me that my case had been transferred to the 8th division of the court. This was the court that would also be hearing the cases of Manouchehr and Akbar Mohammadi. As I left the courtroom I saw my family one last time, but wasn't allowed to talk to them except to say goodbye. I also saw Manouchehr and Akbar with their family. When it was time to go back to Tohid. The guards put Akbar in the same car as the one I rode in. We were made to lie down in a crouched position in the backseat, blindfolded as usual, our seats touching one another. I could see beneath my blindfold that it was Akbar, and we mouthed greetings to one another. We were both happy to see one another, and we drew strength from the knowledge that we were both alive,. As always, Akbar wasn't afraid. I believe that his focus on our goals was very strong, and because of that, he was able to maintain his confidence.

To my great surprise, no more than three or four days later the guards came and took me back to court. This time all three of us, Manouchehr, Akbar, and I, were taken to Section 8 of the Revolutionary Court. Manouchehr and Akbar had agreed to the court-appointed attorneys who had been assigned to them, and we had all been brought to hear the rulings for the two of them. I believe the guards brought me there as another form of psychological torture—to create even more uncertainty about the outcome of my own ruling.

First, Manouchehr was taken from the outer room that was connected to the courtroom. There, Akbar and I listened as the court-appointed attorney admitted complete guilt on the part of his client before asking for the court's mercy. This was particularly maddening for me and the reason I would continue to fight for a private attorney to represent me. The judge announced Manouchehr's sentence of thirteen years imprisonment, and both Akbar and I sighed with relief. His life had been spared, and it wasn't a life sentence. When Manouchehr came back to the outer room, he looked relieved as well, and we both took it as a sign that my sentence would be the same or slightly less.

Next they called Akbar into the courtroom. Before long we heard him yelling at the judge, his angry voice bellowing from the other side of the wall. Manouchehr and I went closer to the door so we could hear what had happened. Akbar had been given the death sentence. Manouchehr and I both walked through the door and into the courtroom where Akbar yelled to the judge, "This is injustice. The young generation will hang you for this ruling." As the VAVAK agents dragged Akbar out of the courtroom and back into the outer room, Akbar screamed, "Long live freedom! Down with dictatorship!"

We followed him back to the outer room, and Manouchehr tried to comfort Akbar. There was a secret service agent in the room with us, and Akbar said that in his life he had fought for his country, volunteering to go to war against Iraq as a teenager. The guard shrugged with a reference to traitors in the Quran.

Back at Tohid that night, I had an interrogation session where we discussed the situation of my representation in court. My main interrogator told me I should have a court-appointed attorney, and I told him, "Yes, look what the court-appointed attorney did for Akbar." I told him that I wanted a public hearing with a jury and my own attorney. This was my right under the Islamic Republic's constitution. My interrogator asked if the hearing only had a few people from my family if that would suffice, and I said no, but that it would be better than nothing.

Less than a week later, I had my own court appearance and my oldest brother and my sister were allowed to attend the hearing. Before going into the courtroom, my brother told me not to worry, that he was working on getting me released. These words that were meant to comfort me were hard to believe given the situation I had been in for the past four months at that point.

When standing before the judge, I mentioned Article 38 of the constitution that forbids torture, and the judge looked puzzled, as if he didn't believe that I had been tortured. Angry, I raised my pant legs to show him my swollen feed and bruised and scratched legs. At that point my brother spoke up, telling the judge that our family would not give up, no matter how much it cost, even though it had cost him his job. At this I was shocked, as it was the first I knew that my brother had lost his job because of my political activities.

I addressed each of the seven charges against me, acting as my own attorney since I was never able to secure representation other than a court-appointed lawyer that I had refused. A few days later, I was moved from Tohid to Evin prison. Akbar was also moved to Evin that same day. Akbar and I were very happy to see one another and to be moved to Evin. I noticed the difficulty with which he walked when we got out of the car. His legs and feet were badly damaged from all the torture. We didn't know it then, but it would be the last time we would see one another. When we got to Evin they separated us, and he was taken to section 209, where he was kept away from the other political prisoners.

I was placed in the quarantine unit where there were drug dealers and other criminals, and I believe my captors thought this experience would be frightening to me. To their disappointment, I'm sure, the experience was very positive for me. I had been raised in a kind of sheltered condition, my father not letting me be exposed to drugs or anyone who was associated with them. But among the prisoners in the quarantine I was treated with respect, and in truth they thought of me as a political hero. What I realized from my time with these men was that they were all human beings who had come from extreme poverty. Poverty had put them in that situation.

I remained in the quarantine area for eleven days until I received vaccinations, and then I was moved to Building #3, which housed political prisoners. Often when past prisoners speak of Evin prison, they refer to it as "the notorious Evin prison." Although Evin certainly is no paradise, compared to Tohid, it is a vast improvement. My experience in Building #3 was like a who's who of political prisoners. By the time I got there, Manouchehr was also there. A few days later, Abbas Amir-Entezam, the activist for whom we had dedicated 4 Khordad, was transferred to Building #3. In those first few days I became reacquainted with Ahmad Batebi of the famed *Economist* photo, holding the bloodied shirt of one of his friend. He reminded me that at the protest of 4 Khordad he had joined our group in demonstrating, and when I was lifted onto the shoulders of members to give a speech, his was one set of shoulders that supported me. We became casual friends during that time, and I felt his heart was in the right place. There were also members of the Mujahadeen Khalq, as well as many student activists. In truth, the influx of student prisoners had given new energy to Building #3. At the time I was there the prisoners were getting along, though I heard later that there was some infighting between them.

Every day at five in the afternoon, we were allowed to go outside for exercise. During that time I would walk with Abbas Amir-Entezam. He would talk to me about his philosophy on the history of the last century in Iran, and I learned to look at many historical events with a different approach. His belief was that the United States had paved the way for much of what our country had experienced in the last fifty years. He believed that President Truman had established three basic tenets that had impacted Iran's place in the world: control of oil, abolishing communism, and establishing peace between the Arabs and the Israelis. He believed that the Islamic Revolution of 1979 was all part of the United State's plan for Iran.

Three and a half weeks after I arrived at Evin, I was told to get ready for another court hearing. When I went before the judge, I was given a sentence of five months in jail, and having already served four in Tohid, and most of the last month in Evin, I would be released within the week. I also had to serve five years of parole, and if I had any political involvement, they would arrest me right away and I'd be taken back to jail.

I was shocked, to say the least. What my brother had told me at that last court hearing before my release from Tohid had been true. He had been working behind the scenes to get me freed.

I went back to Evin, and in truth it was a mixed blessing. On the one hand, I felt grateful that I was being freed, but on the other it was difficult to think of leaving those who had much longer sentences. Manouchehr and the others from our group and from Building #3 were very happy about my release, feeling new hope that I would be able to spread our message outside the walls of the jail, tell the story of what had happened to us, and work to continue our movement in the outside world.

On the day of my release, they gave me the clothes I had been arrested in and my wallet with what little money I had been carrying. As simply as that, I walked outside the walls of Evin prison. I had been warned by those inside to watch out for the Ansar-e Hezbollah, as they would be angry about my release and could easily kill me. I found a payphone outside of Evin and called my family to tell them I was catching a bus home to Mazandaran.

# CHAPTER 7

# THE POWER OF THE STUDENT MOVEMENT

In the news just the other day I read a headline, "Iranian Students Stage Sit-in to Protest Israeli Attacks in Gaza." To the outside world, the reference to "Iranian students" seems to lump us all into one category that is inaccurate at best, and slanderous to a point. The term has as many meanings as there are kinds of students all over the world.

The individuals who took hostages at the U.S. embassy in Tehran in 1979 were referred to as "Iranian students." Present day reference to "Iranian students" ready to martyr themselves for the Palestinian cause bear no resemblance to the students who challenged the Islamic Republic of Iran in July 1999. Yet, even within the ranks of the students who took part in the protests after the dormitory attacks in 1999, there must be a clear delineation between the reformists students (Daftar-e Tahkim-e Vahdat) and the students of The National Union of Iranian Students and Graduates.

The Daftar-e Tahkim-e Vahdat of 1999 were direct descendants of the student organization that was part of the 1979 Revolution in Iran and the hostage taking at the United States embassy. They were also followers of the former president Mohammad Khatami and his reformist platform.

Yet the influence of students in Iran cannot be overlooked. The Iranian student has carried weight in twentieth-century Iranian history. In December 1953, following the coup d'état that overthrew Prime

Minister Mohammad Mossadeqh, students of Tehran University staged a protest in response to American Vice-President Richard Nixon. During the demonstration, the Shah's police shot and killed three students. Students of the day were enraged by the pro-Western Shah's alliance with the United States in the wake of Mossadeqh's overthrow.

Since 1953, December 6 has been celebrated annually as Students Day in Iran. Though the political climate has seen varying kinds of students participating in the events, the significance of student activism in Iran remains an important way of swaying the politics.

The secular student movement in Iran is nothing new to our history. Students have always been at the forefront of Iran's political struggles. Student leaders in Iran's history of the '50s and '60s produced leaders of moderate political organizations that would challenge the Islamic Republic's policy in the early days of the Revolution.

The 1960s and '70s saw both left-leaning intellectual and university students and seminary students in Iran having a prominent role in leading the challenge to the Pahlavi monarchy. Groups like the Iranian People's Fedayee Guerrillas and the Iranian People's Mojahedeen Organization helped overthrow the monarchy in the '70s. Even Khomeini urged an alliance between members of the student movements and the mullahs back then.

For the most part, the student movement in Iran of the '70s was largely secular. They were responsible for initiating some of the most important insurgencies that began the first stages of the Revolution. In the ten largest cities, students organized more than 120 demonstrations against the government of the monarchy. They staged protests and rallies in Tehran and boycotted their classes in opposition to political repression by the government. These events were organized by secular student groups. These same students were the first to come out in protests chanting, "Death to the Shah."

In the months leading up to the Revolution, Tehran's artists and intellectuals were at the forefront of the move toward revolution. They organized nights of poetry readings in opposition to the Shah's government. The outpouring of defiance of the Shah's government and the strength of their presence at protests were so intense that in the fall of 1977, many universities closed before the end of the semester. The government started attacking university campuses, and many students were imprisoned by the Shah's government during that time.

Slowly, the pro-Khomeini student groups grew in number. Many of the students who joined these groups came from small cities throughout Iran and had little experience in student politics—particularly secular politics. In addition to the Islamic students gaining numbers from less politically-inclined students, there was also an influx of Khomeini supporters who joined in their protests from the outside—many of whom were simply infiltrating the Islamic movement at the universities and were not even students. Eventually the religious students were in conflict with the secular students.

On November 4, 1979, with the hostage taking of the U.S. embassy employees by the Islamic students, the student movement of the Islamic Revolution took form in a new way. The religious Muslim Student Followers of the Imam's Line had the attention of the world news, and from all outward appearances they seemed to have the most power in Iran during that time. In truth, the secular students were a far more popular and powerful movement in 1979. This is nowhere more apparent than in the way the government handled non-religious students in the 1980s. The new regime in Iran began the systematic cleansing of Western ideology using the term "cultural revolution," which was taken from the Maoist movement. Students were attacked by government-supported thugs throughout Iran, and the universities were closed for a yet to be determined length of time.

Students became the target of the wrath of the Islamic Republic. From 1981 to 1985, some four thousand students involved in political opposition activities were killed at the hands of the Islamic Republic. Students who were not part of the Islamist groups were either arrested for against the Islamic government or chose to leave the country. By the mid-1980s, the student movement in Iran was made up of religious students.

What the Islamic Republic miscalculated, in my mind, is that all of those who were too young to remember life before the Islamic Republic wouldn't completely buy in to the life presented to us. Even though families were encouraged to rat out their own should a father, mother, or aunt display "un-Islamic" behavior, schools were cleansed of any teachers or literature that espoused anything opposing the Islamic party line, and the media was completely taken over by the Islamic propaganda machine, which found ways of inserting Islam into sports channels as much as news channels, somehow there were still those of us who didn't quite buy it.

What I believe happened to our generation was that we saw the violence that came with the Islamic Revolution and the war with Iraq that quickly followed. Any family that lost a member in jail, having been suspected of any sort of political dissent, didn't completely buy into the Islamic Republic. Any family who sent a son to the Iran-Iraq war only to have him survive and come home to a corrupt government and that kept him from attending university because a dissident uncle was in the Mujahadeen Khalq was left cynical. Anyone from my own generation who spent any time reading the Constitution of the Islamic Republic could shoot so many holes in it that we could hardly be expected to believe it would protect us.

Many from my generation, and especially those of us who were outside of Tehran and had grown up in small villages in middle class families, believed in Iran, but didn't believe that our government was good for our country. This didn't make monarchists of all of us, but it did make us question things. We hated the violence that we had grown used to as part of living in post-Islamic Revolution Iran. After the Iran-Iraq War, we wanted to see peace for our country. Those of us who had a thirst for knowledge understood Iran's history. We wanted a country that provided a separation of religion and government.

When Manouchehr and I traveled outside of Iran that first time, one of the biggest questions we got from Iranians outside the country was, "How can you be secular after living your whole life under the control of the Islamic Republic?" Our responses varied, but the simple truth is that the regime failed my generation. They failed to make us into the devout followers they intended us to be. But that was also perhaps their biggest gift to us.

With all the attention the Islamic Republic paid to protecting their position using a constitution that gives the Supreme Leader and his chosen clergy almost god-like power, what Khomeini and the rest neglected to address was the human spirit. They believed that the people of Iran would follow no matter what. They thought they could brainwash their sons and daughters to believe whatever the regime fed us.

They underestimated us.

Iran's youth has always been at the forefront of change for freedom. Our group, the National Union of Iranian Students and Graduates, was only the beginning of those who questioned the Islamic Republic. We were the first secular student movement after the cultural revolution. We cracked a door open in 1999. Today, students in Iran have fully opened the door, and while they still face violence at the hands of the Islamic Republic, they will not be silenced. It isn't part of our culture to sit down, and Iran's boiling point is at hand. Nowhere has this been more evident than in the reactions to the 2009 re-election of President Mahmoud Ahmadinejad. Using technology like never before—cell phone cameras and video cams to post on Twitter, Facebook, and You Tube—the protesters got the word out to the rest of the world. When the Islamic Republic kicked out foreign media, demonstrators sent images of those being beaten and killed on the streets across the communication wires and outside of Iran

Student movements all over the world have proven to be catalysts for change in the last century. I have always believed that students hold the key to challenge when it comes to social injustices. For one thing, students tend to have an idealistic approach. By this, I don't mean that they are naive, but instead that they have not been beaten down by life yet. As jaded as that might sound, there's truth there. The other thing about students is that they are at the forefront of intellectual stimulation. Universities have always been centers of thought that grow original ideas. While they can tend to be fairly left-leaning, that isn't to say that there aren't student movements that are in many ways more middle-of-the-road than the governments they question.

An example where students were able to stop the world for a time and cause global outrage is the Tiananmen Square protests of 1989 in the People's Republic of China. Just as Ahmad Batebi's photo on the cover of the *Economist* brought him worldwide fame and brought about a global awareness of the student movement in Iran, there is a photo that rivals it taken during the Tiananmen Square protests.

The famous photo depicts a single student standing in front of a row of tanks coming toward him. As the story goes, whenever the tank driver tried to maneuver around the student, the young man would move to block him from going forward. At one point, the student climbed up onto the turret of the lead tank to speak to the soldiers inside. Stories vary about what he said, but once he climbed down, he was escorted away by People's Republic of China secret police. Cameras caught the image and it has become an icon for the strength students have in the world. What happened to the young man for certain has never been established. Some say he was executed right away, while others report that he was able to escape and go into hiding. Whatever his outcome, his image will live on forever.

The Chinese students during the Tiananmen Square protests were demonstrating against the PRC's authoritarian rule and mourning the death of a pro-democracy official, Hu Yaobang. The protests lasted for six weeks, and ended with a reported two to three thousand students being killed. They didn't overthrow the government, but they did cause the government of the People's Republic of China to take pause. They also got the attention of the rest of the world in their brave struggle for freedom.

Examples of student uprising that have had major impacts on how governments behaved abound all over the world. Almost every corner of the globe has examples of students risking their academic careers and sometimes their lives to make a point. The 1960s proved to be tumultuous times where the youth of the age stood up against the establishment in ways that changed the way governments reacted to their youth. While many of the governments would not take the opportunity to self-reflect in the wake of the events, years later their impact would be recognized throughout the world.

On October 2, 2008, some forty thousand people came out into the streets of Mexico City to mark the fortieth anniversary of the student protests of 1968, known as the Tlatelolco massacre. Demonstrators carried signs that read, "Yo no estuvo alli, pero no olvido," which translates as, "I wasn't there, but I won't forget." Those who participated drew chalk outlines of the dead bodies of students that had lain in the streets in 1968.

That year the Summer Olympics were to be held in Mexico City. It would be the first time the event had taken place in a Latin American country, and the stakes were high to make the event safe and free from controversy.

University students seized the opportunity to demonstrate for a set of demands that included freedom for political prisoners, the right for groups to meet, and taking authorities to task for violence by tactical police groups against citizens.

The students began their demonstrations in the months before the 1968 Olympic Games were to begin. On October 2, 1968, the numbers of student protestors wearing red carnations grew to some fifteen thousand students marching through the streets of Mexico City. That evening around five thousand of them remained in the Plaza de las Tres Culturas in Tlatelolco when military and police forces surrounded the square. The students were mercilessly attacked. The government's version of the story was that students began sniper-like shooting at the police forces, causing the government troops to engage in returned gunfire. While the estimated on the number of lives lost in the massacre varies, it has been reported that between two and three hundred students were killed that day.

In 2001, an investigation into the massacre found that the snipers were in fact members of the Presidential Guard who were instructed to stage a sniper attack that would justify the shooting by the military. In a 2003 report by the U.S. government, records indicated that the Pentagon had supplied Mexico with military radios, weapons, ammunition, and riot control training material for the attack and had put pressure on the Mexican government to settle the student uprisings before the Olympic Games began.

The price students in Mexico paid was heavy, but the legacy they left forty years later is no less powerful. They didn't change a regime, but they clearly made enough noise to incite not one, but two governments to act. How they were gunned down is no less tragic, yet it demonstrates the level of fear the students had engendered.

Fear was the order of the day in the 1960s when it came to students. Nowhere is that more apparent than the student movement in the United States and the formation of the Students for a Democratic Society (SDS). The SDS was a student movement that challenged the entire political system of the United States in its manifesto, The Port Huron Statement. In a report entitled "Restless Youth," former CIA director Richard Helms expressed that fear when encouraging President Lyndon B. Johnson to authorize the FBI to dive deeper into the activities of what he termed "young radicals" in the United States. The United States government was convinced that outside communist organizations were empowering the youth of the country. With an approach that was decidedly left-leaning, though not communist, the SDS favored a rejection of the anti-communist politics that was so prevalent in 1960s and 1970s United States politics. Try as they may, the government must have been disappointed to find little evidence of outside influence into the SDS.

The SDS was based on the idea of nonviolent civil disobedience. It was founded by young, middle-class university students who were concerned about the future they would inherit. The SDS was important because it provided a valuable example of how a student movement has to insert itself into as many universities across the country as possible. In this way, SDS was able to gain a critical mass that challenged the status quo. In my mind, this is what the SDS did very well. In an essay written by Tom Hayden during the Clinton administration, he discusses how SDS was able to push the government of the '60s to make changes. Hayden was one of the founders of SDS and drafted the Port Huron Statement.

Of the changes that took effect as a result of student presence in peaceful protests, the most notable was that the Vietnam War troops began to be brought home in 1969. During that same time, the compulsory military draft also ended. More than either of these, however, my thoughts on what the '60s student movements in the United States and Europe—France and Germany in particular—represented was an overall political and cultural shift.

The Port Huron Statement is important because it begins with a very strong statement about the value of our humanity. While this may seem soft in some ways, espousing a mutual love between humankind, but in truth this was a very important statement, and one that is in line with any movement that holds human rights dear. What I mean by this is that the basis for SDS was beyond anything that the United States was prepared to combat, and the idea of respect for humanity and ending what they considered an imperial war was profound in its simplicity.

The SDS of the 1960s ended as an organization with a final convention in 1969. There were several factors that led to its ultimate undoing, but perhaps the largest was the complexity of the time. There was much to fight for during those years, with civil rights, women's rights, and labor rights, to name a few, all fighting for a place at the table. But their legacy was that they opened the door for other movements while working their own agendas.

South Korea has a long history of students making a difference within the government. In the twentieth century, students had a very strong presence in resistance during the Japanese occupation from 1910 to 1945. Just as the 1960s proved to be a powerful decade for other student movements all over the world, South Korean students were instrumental in overthrowing the autocratic First Republic of South Korea under Syngman Rhee in April 1960.

Following a protest in the wake of an election that was fraudulent, some one thousand citizens came out into the streets of Mazan, Korea. Days later the body of a student protester was found washed up on the beach of Masan. The student, Kim Ju-yul, had been killed by the shell of a tear gas grenade.

Students in Seoul came out to march from Korea University to the presidential mansion, increasing in numbers along the way. While it is unclear how many students stood at the gates of Korea's Blue House presidential mansion, it is clear that they infuriated President Syngman Rhee, who had his soldiers begin shooting. Some 125 students were killed that day, April 19, 1960. The result was the eventual resignation of the president of Korea and a transition to a new government.

What South Korean's April Revolution, as it was called, meant to the student movement, though the cost was great, was that change could happen when the government was faced head on.

Another event in South Korea that demonstrated the strength of their student movement is the Gwangju Democratization Movement in 1980. On May 18 of that year, students demonstrated against the closure of the Chonnam National University. Three days later, the protests escalated and the result was vicious attacks by the military police. Casualties were high, but what started as student demonstrations paved the way for later movements in the 1980s that would eventually bring democracy to South Korea.

Years later, many of these same student activists would become known as the "386 Generation." The 386 Generation consists of South Koreans who were in their thirties in the 1990s, attended universities in the 1980s, and were born in the 1960s. Credited with transforming the government of South Korea in the 1980s, 386ers would go on to be credited for spreading democracy within the country. They demanded greater economic equality and more social justice.

While some argue that the 386ers who went on to political careers within the government have not delivered what their idealist youth had promised, their roles in changing the government cannot be ignored. They were instrumental in ushering in a democracy that still exists today.

There are countless other examples of student movements that have contributed to change within repressive regimes. Indonesia's students were part of what eventually led to a revolution in 1998 that overthrew the dictatorship of President Suharto. The pressure they put on the government through protests caused the eventual resignation of the Indonesian president. Students have also had a strong presence the Burmese struggle, and students in the Philippines have a very active place in the history of their government. What becomes a central theme throughout all these struggles is that at some point, the cost in human life is often the catalyst that spurs the change.

This is no different from what our own movement in Iran has shown. Whether it has been through attacks like the one we endured in the dormitories of Tehran University in 1999 or street massacres in the streets of Mexico City or South Korea, the sacrifices are unfortunate realities.

While most student movements share a common vision, there are distinct differences between issues and countries. One of the biggest differences comes in the concept of Third World vs. First World activism. In First World countries, the accomplishments of students are no less, but still there's a difference. Coming from a First World mentality, the fight can be more systematic. There is freedom to question—a right many in the Third World do not enjoy.

Additionally, it is difficult to compare issues between the Third and First World. For example, a fight because of increases in university fees is somewhat different than a struggle to fight imperialism so that peasants have running water and sanitation, as is the case in many Latin American and other Third World countries.

In Iran, we are fighting for our lives. We have been brutalized by violence and fanaticism, and we have risen with strength and will that is part of our culture. We have seen too many of our young people hanging from gallows senselessly. We have been jailed and tortured, and our families have had to watch their children be tormented.

What we can learn, however, is how others have succeeded in movements in First World countries. We can take the tools and mold them to work for Iran and other Third World countries. We learn from the past, and in this we have the audacity to believe that change is not only possible, but it is certain.

# CHAPTER 8

# ESCAPE FROM IRAN

Mazandaran Province sits at the base of the Alborz Mountains and looks north toward the Caspian Sea. It is green and has weather that is temperate. As I rode a bus north to my home, my eyes were so full of wonder at the land that I didn't know I would ever see again. My feeling at that time is difficult to explain. While one might think that I would be completely overjoyed, in truth I felt immense sadness as I looked out the window at the mountains, seeing the dense forest that surrounds them.

I thought of those I had left in Evin prison, but I also thought of those who had lost their battles with the Islamic regime, those who died in Tohid and Evin prisons, and thousands more like them all over the world. During my time in Tohid, I could feel the memory of so many who had died there. It was as if they left an imprint somehow, and in the dark hours of my imprisonment, I could feel their loneliness, their hopelessness, and their pain.

During my time in Evin prison, along the baseboard of one of the walls next to the showers in the quarantine area, I will never forget the writing left by a female prisoner from sometime past. It is forever etched in my memory. The quote was a note left for her friend, and it said, "Hamideh, tonight is the last night of my life. Tell Alireza to take care of our children." I imagined this woman wondering if her children would ever know how she thought of them until the very end. I wished that I knew how to find Alireza, who must have been her husband. I wished that I could tell their children that they should never have lost their mother.

As the bus neared my home city, Babol, I breathed deeply, trying to put the past few months behind me, present a positive face to my family, and then begin planning for the next move for the student movement. From the bus stop I walked to my house, and already there were people from our town waiting to greet me. These were the people from my neighborhood and the small town around our house, Ahangar Kolah. A couple of the men grabbed me and put me on their shoulders, parading me around in front of our house, while the women and children clapped and cheered. These were common people, and this was their reaction to what the government had done to one of their sons. I saw that they didn't agree with the regime, and this was how they showed us their support. There were families who had lost children who were part of the Mujahedeen Khalq or socialists, and they were there to support my mother and the return of her son.

Over the next several weeks, people came from seven in the morning until the afternoon to see me. Most of them had read about my case in the newspaper, and they came to give me their support. Our generation of the student movement had given new energy to the idea of changing the regime. People trusted our beliefs and were happy to see the youth of our country taking a stand.

During the time I spent in Mazandaran, my mother and Arash slept with me every night. My mother stayed very close to me, afraid that if she wandered very far from my side, she might lose me again. My time in prison had been particularly hard on her. When she saw my image broadcast on television, she thought I was as good as gone forever. Now, she clung to me as much as she could, and I didn't blame her for that.

After I was home for two days, I decided to go to Manouchehr and Akbar's hometown, Amol, to see their parents. They were happy to see me, and were working to get their sons released.

Two weeks later I returned to Tehran and started making contact with members of our group who had been released from jail or had somehow avoided arrest. I met with Rihaneh Hashemi, her daughter, and several others from our group, and we decided that we needed to rebuild the organization from the ground up.

When in Tehran, I couldn't forget the months I had spent at Tohid, and it became a kind of obsession for me to find the location of the prison. When I was in Tohid on one of the top level floors, I could hear a bell that seemed to ring at certain hours of the day, though I wasn't sure when it was because my sense of time was so confused. I imagined then that the prison was close to a church. After comparing notes with other students who had gone there, we determined that the bell was not a church, but instead was a local bank. Based on what we all recalled, we were able to piece together our findings and discover the location of Tohid prison. It would be several months before I would make that knowledge public.

The remaining free members of our group set out to rebuild our organization, and we began by sending a press release to newspapers and radio stations inside and outside of Iran. The release announced that our group was still intact, what had happened after July 1999, that our members had been persecuted, thrown in jail, and endured the worst of the wrath of the Islamic Republic. Our operations were more secret than they had been before, and for this reason I traveled back and forth between Northern Iran and Tehran as much as possible.

As I have said, the Mohammadis were working to get both of their sons released, and they had been sent word from the Revolutionary Court that the only way their case would be heard was if I were to attend the hearing. This came directly from the head of the Revolutionary Court, Hojatoleslam Gholamhossein Rahbarpour. On the day of the court hearing, I met Manouchehr and Akbar's parents at the court. When we appeared in front of Rahbarpour, he pointed to me and announced to the Mohammadis, "This is the person who has the key to the release of your sons. If he has an interview with either *Kehan* or *Ettelaat* newspaper, and says that their student group was wrong, and if he apologizes to the government, we will release your sons." At this, Mrs. Mohammadi started to cry.

Rahbarpour had put me in a very compromising position. If I agreed to the interview with one of the conservative newspapers, because I was out of jail and not being tortured, my reputation would be forever tarnished. The suspicion that I was with the regime would be almost impossible to ever disprove. He knew this very well. If I refused to apologize, my friends continued to suffer in Evin prison, and

I contributed to their parents' already broken hearts. When we left the courts, I turned to Mr. Mohammadi and said, "I can't do what they are asking of me." He looked sad, but he replied that he understood, and that whatever I thought was right he would trust.

After that interaction with the Revolutionary Court, members of our group became worried about my safety. In truth we all knew that it was only a matter of time before the Islamic regime put me back in jail or worse. There was an overall feeling that I would do more good for our movement if I went to Europe or the United States. In truth, I really didn't want to leave Iran. In time, however, I became convinced that I would be more effective at growing our movement if I had the freedom of the press behind me as I would in a Western country. I would follow Forouhar's advice and leave the country.

I left Iran in May 2000. I hadn't planned extensively, and left the country with very little money. I had contacted several people who I knew had connections, and so that I don't compromise any of them, I'll only say that the wheels were set in motion so that I was able to board a jet on Turkish Airlines, and fly from Tehran using my Islamic Republic of Iran passport. Every step of my trip I expected at any moment to be arrested and sent back to jail, but it was as if I were invisible. No one recognized me from television or newspapers, and my name clearly written on my passport rang no bells. Iranians traveling to Turkey do not require visas, so I walked through customs in Turkey without incident. The escape from Iran was surreal in its ease.

Once in Turkey, I found a small room and from there made contact first with Hossein Mohri of Sedaye Iran radio in Los Angeles. Mr. Mohri had been one of our primary voices outside Iran during all our protests, and Sedaye Iran Radio had become quite famous due to its support of the student movement during that time.

After I contacted Mr. Mohri, I called Mehdi Jaferi Gorzini, a member of the Green Party in Meinz, Germany, Majid Rooshanzadeh, who was the student president of Freie Universität in Germany, and Nasrin Basiri, who had previously interviewed me for Radio Multi Culti in Berlin. Jaferi Gorzini, Rooshanzadeh, and Basiri worked together to decide the best way for me to proceed. Rooshanzadeh was able to secure financial support for me through Freie Universität.

I stayed in Turkey for several weeks. The reasons I didn't leave for Europe were complicated. As we approached the first anniversary of July 1999, it was also the timing that Iran's President Khatami was planning a visit to Germany. While Freie Universität was willing to support me financially, their preference, along with the Green Party and the Heinrich Boll Foundation of Germany, was that I stay in Turkey until after Khatami's visit. None of them were keen on the idea of students rioting, as much as they supported my cause.

During that time, Nasrin Basiri had connections with Germany's largest weekly magazine, *Der Spiegel*, and they wanted to come to Turkey to interview me. They wanted to do a story to find out why the Green Party had invited me before, but now wouldn't support me making a visit to Germany. Finally, my visa to Germany was approved and by mid-June I flew to Berlin from Istanbul. I had the interview with *Der Spiegel* at that time.

I stayed for ten days with Majid Rooshanzadeh in Berlin before going back to Meinz to stay with Mehdi Jaferi Gorzini. In all truth I was unsure what to do for the anniversary of July 1999. I decided to have a press conference in Frankfurt, and I published an open letter to Mohammad Khatami that was published on the Iran Press Service and on various other Web sites in German, French, Farsi, and English. In the letter I announced the beginning of a hunger strike by students still imprisoned in Evin prison and led by Manouchehr. It was also in this letter that I made the location of Tohid prison public knowledge.

Until I was outside the walls of that terrible place, I couldn't really put a name to it. It was only after being released and finding the exact location that I knew I had been in Tohid, one of the most notorious prisons that had ever existed in Iran. In the letter I referred to a book written by the Supreme Leader Ali Khamenei, in which he describes several days he spent in Tohid at the hands of the Shah's regime. Khamenei said of his time in Tohid that it was the most bitter and dreadful period of his life. In my letter to President Khatami, I said, "And yet, the atmosphere and conditions that existed there at that time were much better than they are now, and we spent 136 days in that same place, in conditions much more horrific, and have endured the harshest torture."

One day after I published the letter to Khatami, the Majlis in Iran released a story that they had just discovered the existence of Tohid prison and that they were closing its doors. The discovery of Tohid prison couldn't have been very difficult for the regime, since they had been using it to house political prisoners for the past twenty years at that point. Darker than Evin prison, Tohid was a virtual torture chamber, where atrocities occurred that rivalled the worst of such places anywhere in the world. Following the transfer of ownership of Tohid from the Shah's time, I heard that the Islamic Republic of Iran made changes to the prison, dividing some of the rooms so as to accommodate more prisoners. Today Tohid is a museum in remembrance of those who were imprisoned there during the time of the Shah of Iran.

On the actual anniversary of July 1999, several thousand students came out to protest at Tehran University, the student prisoners still at Evin began their hunger strike, and I gave a press conference in Frankfurt where I again mentioned Tohid.

The next day, President Khatami came to Berlin. All my contacts from Iran and Europe had Mehdi's mobile number as the means to contact me, but on that same day access to Mehdi's cell phone was cut. I was unable to receive communication for the next few days. We believed at that time that the government of Germany had disabled the mobile number during Khatami's trip so that there would be no protests during his visit.

Following the anniversary of July 1999, members of VAVAK paid a visit to my family in Babol. They threatened that because I had left Iran and made problems for the regime that they would find me, and warned that they could reach me even outside the country.

I stayed in Germany for a few more months, and once my tourist visa to the United States was approved, I decided that I would move to there to continue my work for our organization. My reasoning for moving to Los Angeles was that I felt it had the strongest Iranian media and there many Iranian people there to help start building our movement in the United States.

I landed in Los Angeles, California, with sixty dollars in my wallet. I found a Motel 6 close to the airport and started making calls as soon as I landed. I had previously made contact with the Mission for Establishing Rights in Iran (MEHR) organization, and their president,

Dr. Mohammad Parvin, put me in touch with some of his supporters who were willing to help me find my way in the United States. MEHR was a particularly appealing organization for me because they focused on human rights for Iran, but they tried not to choose sides politically. This would prove particularly valuable as I got to know the political landscape of L.A. and the Persian community.

Once in L.A., I started working on building our student group outside Iran right away. Whether it was ignorance at how the system worked with Iranian media in Los Angeles, enthusiasm, or blind faith, I started working on my politics with complete confidence as soon as I landed in southern California. I began interviewing on a regular basis with Sedaye Iran radio. The Islamic regime was able to pick up their signal and it was the way I could communicate my activities to the students in our group back home.

Next I started touring different universities that had invited me to speak. I traveled to University of California, Berkeley, and was invited to Dartmouth College in New Hampshire by Dr. Misagh Parsa. Dr. Hamid Akbari invited me to Northwestern University in Chicago twice, and I made a couple of trips to Washington, D.C., where I made contact with other students as well. My plan at that time was to gather as many young Iranians as possible and organize our group. I founded the International Alliance of Iranian Students and found a Web developer who was willing to build our first Web site. Our mailing list grew very quickly from our contact page and we were well on our way to building a community of Iranian students outside of Iran.

While it looked like I was progressing toward achieving my goal, I hit the first of many snags with the Los Angeles Iranian community. The United States has the largest number of Iranians outside of Iran. In L.A., it is estimated that the Iranian population is as high as one million people. The make-up of the Iranian population in Los Angeles grew largely out of the 1979 Islamic Revolution. The early '80s saw an increase in Iranians immigrating to the United States, and of those, many are Iranian monarchists.

As I have said, the early reception by Iranian monarchists was fairly positive. They accepted me and Manouchehr when we first visited, and they supported us through the months following our return to Iran. Once I landed in the United States, the monarchists were willing to have me participate in their events, but the idea of me blazing my own trail and not following their political agenda made waves right away.

The fact that the Iranian media in Los Angeles had grown out of the events of July 1999 represented something we had both done for one another. In their minds, however, they owned the news, and they wanted control of it once I was in L.A. Sticking to my political goals and not succumbing to the temptation to change my ideology was still very much my political stance. I had come too far, standing up to the Islamic Republic and paying the price of not having Manouchehr, Akbar, and others freed, to let the Iranians in L.A. change me.

In the beginning, I tried to be united with the monarchists. We had many points of common interest. They were secular. They hated the Islamic Republic's regime as much as I did. But it was important to stay independent from them because our group had grown out of the idea of a secular democracy that was focused more on the ideas of Mohammad Mossadeqh. The idea of bringing a royal family back to rule Iran was not in line with my beliefs or the beliefs of our members in Iran. If I aligned with the monarchists, I gave the appearance of endorsing their political views for Iran in the future.

We finally clashed for real over the approach to the second anniversary of July 1999. The monarchists had planned the entire event, and when I got up to speak I made a point to state that I was independent. During my speech, the sound system continually failed, so that the sound was spotty at best. The rest of the demonstration had a distinct feel of the movement being based on the monarchists' platform.

I didn't say anything after the event, but I made a decision that the third anniversary of July 1999 would be different. For the next twelve months I would work tirelessly. I would spend every waking hour networking and building our group. I lived on very little money and rarely relaxed or did anything that would be considered recreational. In truth, I was on a mission. I knew what the prisoners at Evin still endured every day, and it pulled at me all the time.

I decided to plan the third anniversary of July 1999. I started researching what it would take to pull a demonstration off, taking control of the event from the beginning. I got a permit to demonstrate on July 8, 2001 in front of the Federal Building in downtown Los Angeles. It wasn't long until the word got out that I was planning the event, and I started receiving invitations to meet with the Iranian monarchists to discuss my plans.

We met on a couple occasions, the most memorable of which was in Westwood. The event was led by the head of Sadaye Iran radio in Los Angeles, Assadollah Morovati. Morovati held quite a bit of power in Los Angeles, and he was backed up by previous generals from Iran and other media power brokers. The message was clear: have the July 1999 anniversary with the monarchists or lose media support all together. I refused. The meeting became heated. My feeling was that maintaining support in Iran was more important than having the support of the media in Los Angeles.

Now, to be fair, it's important to note that not all Iranians in Los Angeles are monarchists, and not everyone agrees with them. It must also be said that not all monarchists behave the same way, and many have very similar desires for Iran as our group did. Because the Iranian monarchists have power, however, they are a force to be reckoned with. Also, a town like Los Angeles can change people culturally, and most of the people who I was dealing with had been there for more than twenty years. Culturally, the Iranian monarchists had become something other than the Iranians who left our country two decades before. They had learned to survive in a very difficult place, and they had made it. They were used to doing things a certain way, and here I was, this new kid of whom some were still suspicious since I came from a movement created inside Iran and was able to escape the government there.

Finally, after arguing the point until neither side would budge, I left the meeting, telling themthat I was having the anniversary of July 1999 on the same day as others in our movement were having it in Iran and Europe, and that it would be in front of the Federal Building in downtown Los Angeles. The next day, stories came out about me in the Persian press in Los Angeles. They reported that I had always been suspicious, as if I had been sent by the Islamic Republic regime, and that I couldn't be trusted. They went on to state that I drove a Mercedes Benz and have a house in Beverly Hills. This was so far from the truth it was laughable. I barely had two nickels to rub together and I lived on very little, sending any small amount of money that came my way back to Iran to help the students in our group.

The bottom line with my falling out with the Iranian monarchists in 2001 was that they felt they should have control, and I refused to send the message that I had the same political ideas as they did. I don't believe I would handle the situation any differently today if I had it to do over. In truth, today I believe there are those from that time who know they would have been better off supporting our group almost a decade ago.

Without the support of the Iranian media in Los Angeles, getting the word out was a challenge. We used the approach we had used when doing demonstrations at Tehran University, printing flyers that our new members of the International Alliance of Iranian Students passed out at Persian markets and other places of business frequented by Iranians in Los Angeles.

On July 8, 2001, we had a turnout of some eight thousand people in front of the Federal Building in Los Angeles. Amnesty International was there, as was one of the attorneys I had requested while in prison, Mehrangiz Kar. Mehrangis Kar is a very well-known women's right activist, and had been arrested in January of that year, but was temporarily released when doctors discovered she had developed cancer. At the time, she was in the United States receiving treatment for her illness, but her husband was jailed in Iran. We also had Iranian feminist and researcher of political science and women's studies, Janet Afary, give a speech.

At one point during Mehrangis Kar's speech, a group of monarchists attacked the stage. From where I sat, it was like watching the Ansar-e Hezbollah all over again. They screamed that Kar was from the regime, and I was shocked that we would see such hatred in the United States from our own expatriates. There were police and FBI agents there at the protest, and they immediately arrested the two leaders of the attack. The monarchists who were there had wanted to have some of their people give speeches, but I had a set agenda and I refused them. I believe this was what led to the outbreak. As soon as I saw the police begin arresting the two, I asked that they be released, which they were.

The outcome of that day was that the new student organization that had organized the anniversary, International Alliance of Iranian Students, had held an independent gathering. For twenty years the Iranian monarchists had held all the power in the Iranian community, and this was the first time any other group was able to have power. In the following days we were not surprised to see that the Iranian media hadn't covered any of the activities of the day. The only reference was in follow-up stories to the ones they had published in the weeks before the demonstrations, again accusing me of coming from the regime and having a house in Beverly Hills and a Mercedes.

Though we had been successful, at the end I felt a kind of sadness that we had so much disagreement among us. How could we ever make the adjustments necessary to change the government in our beloved Iran if we couldn't support one another outside the country? I was hurt that they sunk to the level of making up lies about me.

The Persian media, however, were not done with me after the third anniversary of July 1999. They went on to make contact with members of the National Union of Iranian Students and Graduates inside Iran, and told them that student members there could either support me or have media support in Los Angeles from the Iranian community there. While most of the students in Iran who were part of our group understood my position and stayed strong in their support, this caused several of our students to break ties with me.

As I reflect on that time, I realize that to some degree the events that took place in the summer of 2001 took some of my newcomer brazenness away. After that, I chose to slow down some of my activity and start focusing on finding my path in the United States. Up to that point, I lived physically in the United States, but my heart was always in Iran. For the good of our movement and so that I could regain the strength I needed to continue, I had to take some time for myself to recuperate.

# CHAPTER 9

# SEPTEMBER 11, 2001

Like almost every person who lived on U.S. soil on 9/11, I will remember the moment of finding out about the attacks for as long as I live. On the morning of September 11, 2001, I got a call from a friend who told me a war had begun and to turn on the news. I was living in Encino, California, at the time, renting a room while doing odd jobs to support myself while continuing my political work.

In all honesty, my first thought was, "God, I hope they weren't Iranians." I think most minorities in this country hoped their particular group wasn't involved in such a heinous act. As the news progressed over the next several days, and as we started piecing together the images of the nineteen hijackers who flew jets into the strategic targets on the east coast of the United States, we learned that Al Quaeda was responsible. I knew that whoever it was, they had to be religious fanatics. For example, a socialist group wouldn't have chosen suicide missions to make a point.

What 9/11 did to the world can never be undone. Personally, I knew almost immediately that our movement would be impacted because there would be an immediate shift in priorities all over the world. I started calling friends in Iran from various cities all over the country, and the concern from them was overwhelming. They all wanted to know more than what they heard on the news, and thought because I was in the United States I would have better information than they had, which I didn't.

In Iran, people were very saddened by the attacks. During a soccer match in Tehran's Azadi Stadium, some sixty thousand spectators observed a moment of silence in memory of those who perished. At Friday prayers, for the first time since the Islamic Revolution of 1979, the chants of "death to America" ceased on the Friday following September 11. On September 18, 2001, citizens of Tehran came out into the streets to hold a candlelight vigil for the loss of life caused by the religious extremists who attacked the United States.

Shortly after that, the secret police paid a visit to my family home in Mazandaran. They told my family to send a message to me that as a nationalist, and as someone who cared about his country, I should cease any lobbying against Iran during this time. They came in the capacity of "caring fellow citizens" and were almost kind to my family. I think they were unsure of how the United States was going to react in the wake of the attacks on New York and Washington D.C., and knew that dissidents like me could help to build a case against the country.

In truth, I was concerned for Iran. While I have always wanted change in my country from the religious fundamentalists who have controlled it since 1979, I believe that change has to come from the inside and without outside influence or violence. I believe that we need moral support from outside Iran, but it is up to Iranians to change the government. The idea of an imposed democracy was not something I wanted for my country. Iranians had to *want* the change for it to stick, and it should come with as little bloodshed as possible.

In President George W. Bush's State of the Union address in January 2002, the administration lumped Iran together with Iraq and North Korea in his now famous "Axis of Evil" speech. In his speech, Bush accused Iran of "aggressively pursuing" weapons of mass destruction and exporting terror. By that time, the United States had already attacked Afghanistan in their attempt to capture Osama bin Laden. During the beginning of that offensive, Iran had offered logistical assistance to the United States in dealing with Afghanistan and had even offered use of its territory bordering Afghanistan for the United States to carry out search and rescue missions. The Islamic Republic had a long-standing dislike of the Taliban and was more than happy to assist in taking them out of power. Even they didn't agree with the level of fundamentalism for which the Taliban were famous. The Taliban are extremely anti-

Shiite, and the Islamic Republic of Iran has a Shia majority. In addition to that, in 1998 the Taliban were responsible for the killing of eleven Iranian diplomats in Afghanistan—an event that almost caused a war between Iran and Afghanistan at the time.

After January 2002, the walls of distrust went back up and the chance for dialogue between Iran and the United States all but disappeared. In response to the Axis of Evil speech, Iran's Foreign Minister Kamal Kharrazi released the following statement, "We condemn the American accusations and think the world no longer accepts hegemony. We think Mr. Bush would do better by providing proof of his allegations."

In the spring of 2002, I moved back to Washington, D.C. for a couple of months. At that time I had a close friend who acted as a translator for me since my English was still not very strong. My translator had ties in the Capitol and was contacted by U.S. Senator Brownback from Kansas, asking for a chance to meet with me. Senator Brownback is a Republican, and he was working at that time on gaining support for Senate Resolution 82 and the amendment to the FY '04 Foreign Relations Authorization Act in the Senate Foreign Relations Committee. The amendment, known as the "Iran Democracy Act," would provide fifty million dollars in funding for an "Iran Democracy Foundation."

Senator Brownback wanted to meet with me as a member of the student movement in Iran because he wanted me to go before the U.S. Senate to voice my support of this amendment. From the outside, the bill looked very appealing, but as I looked more closely, I saw that it was supported by the Iranian monarchists and would benefit their broadcasting efforts.

As I learned more I became certain that I wanted no part of the Iran Democracy Foundation. I respectfully declined Senator Brownback's offer to go before the Senate, and he was shocked. He asked me about the work I did, and wanted to know how I financially supported myself, and suggested that this foundation would help someone like me. I explained to him that whatever financial support was put into an effort to democratize Iran, it needed to come from Iranian support, and Iranian funding. I told him that ultimately, the passing of his amendment would hurt those inside Iran who were fighting for freedom. The Islamic Republic would see the amendment as an attempt at overthrow, and they would be even harder on the students who worked there—especially if they had any contact at all with anyone in the United States.

My view was that this amendment and funding would give the Iranian-American monarchists the power they so desperately wanted, and inside Iran it would sabotage the work that pro-democracy groups had spent years building.

I spent more than two hours in Senator Brownback's office. In the end I thanked him for the opportunity to talk to him, but let him know that culturally, his approach was not in line with what I believed was right for my country.

Later that year, the U.S. House of Representatives passed a non-binding version of the Iran Freedom and Democracy Support Act. A similar version of the act had already been introduced and passed in the Senate. However, neither version included allocation of the fifty million dollars.

In June 2003, the students at Tehran University and other universities inside Iran started an uprising that some thought could be bigger than the July 1999 protests. The issue they protested had to do with a fee increase, and in my mind I honestly didn't think this would escalate to the extent the protests after the dorm attacks in 1999 did. After 1999, the Islamic Republic was more prepared for student protests due to what they had experienced with our group. They understood how to control the situation better by 2003.

During that same time, my interpreter in Washington, D.C., called me very excited. He had received a call from the White House, and they wanted to support me with a press conference to tell the Iranian students that they had "our" support. I would be the face in front of the camera, but the backdrop would be the White House official press room. Again, I felt that this would put me in conflict with my mission to stay independent, and making a statement in front of the American flag that "we" were supporting the students sounded problematic on many levels to me. I felt if I did the press conference, it would put more distance between me and the Iranian students, and based on the prevailing image of the United States calling Iran "the axis of evil," I could hardly see how that support would send the right message. In some ways, it rang of military support from the United States, which was the last thing I wanted for my country. The idea of a military strike by the United States that could kill countless civilians didn't sound like my kind of support.

I responded to my interpreter that I appreciated the offer, but would have to think about it. I needed to go back to Los Angeles, as we were again having the anniversary of July 1999 at the Federal Building. This would be the third anniversary. My interpreter didn't take my response well. He became angry and told me that I didn't understand what a huge opportunity was being offered to me. I did understand the opportunity, but I believed that accepting support from in inappropriate source was worse than not taking the opportunity at all.

I returned to Los Angeles a week before our demonstration at the Federal Building. That year we had collaborated with organizations in thirteen cities all over the world. We all marked the anniversary of July 1999 during the weekend of July 6 and 7. Other than Los Angeles, the other cities to participate were: Washington D.C., London, Athens, Hamburg, Berlin, Frankfurt, Stockholm, Amsterdam, Oslo, Nicosia, Paris, and Brussels.

In Los Angeles, the speakers included famous Iranian poet Ishmael Hooey and Iranian historian Bahram Moshiri. I also made a speech to mark the occasion. The Los Angeles Iranian media didn't cover the demonstration at all. We did get coverage by the English press in the United States, including the *Los Angeles Times* and the *Washington Times*.

The Persian media had started working to undermine any work that I did, and it was causing disagreements between me and other members of our group, not to mention with other organizations, like Tabarzadi's.

This period began what would be close to four years of political silence from me. While I had minimal presence within groups who continued working, my voice as a leader took a backseat for a number of reasons. After 9/11, the hope for regime change in Iran that wasn't precipitated by military force from the United States or another Western power had all but vanished. I saw at that time that as a group, we were going to have to wait for the right time to push forward. The whole world was looking at Afghanistan and later at Iraq, and the student movement in Iran took a hit for the circumstances going on globally.

I told friends in Iran who supported me that the time wasn't right for the student movement. We would continue to exist, but we would wait until the climate was better to push forward. Our group inside and outside of Iran did continue, but to a lesser degree. Many new students were coming out of Iran and seeking asylum in Europe, and I helped their cases by writing letters in support of the work they had done in Iran, and why they should receive political asylum.

I ceased to fight the Persian media in Los Angeles, but I also didn't do any political work there. It is important to note that other than Iran, Los Angeles, which has been termed "Tehran-angeles" due to how many Persians live and work there, is the most important hub for Iranians in the world. Not doing political work there took me out of politics.

Along with all these reasons to go silent, the truth was that I needed to take the time to figure out how to "live" in the United States. Since none of my academic work had transferred to the United States, and even if it had I had no transcripts left from my studies in Iran, I needed to go back to school, and that meant starting from the beginning. My English needed attention, and without a degree, I would not be able to achieve my goals in the future in Iran.

In Iran, one of the foremost of cultural values is education. Of the immigrants to the United States, they are one of the most educated groups, and they tend to do very well in academics outside the country. Though there was a death warrant on my head should I return to Iran, I believed that one day, the regime would change. Whatever part I played in that change, my hope was that one day I would return to my country and do good work for the people of Iran. Whether it was founding a school for underprivileged or building a university, without completing my education, nothing would be possible. A bachelor's degree wouldn't be the end, either. I would need to go on and receive a Masters at least, but most likely I would need a PhD.

Finding a way to support myself and return to school would prove to be a huge challenge. I went to work doing any odd job I could, and tried on several occasions to return to school full-time. I managed to piece together a few college credits here and there, but survival in the United States was more difficult than I had imagined. During this time one of my friends from Iran and a past member of our group, Hamid Alizadeh, came to the United States. We had long talks about what was going on inside of Iran, and though I wasn't politically active at that time, seeing him reminded me that eventually I would go back to work toward my goal in the student movement. The time we spent together reinforced my decision to focus on my education.

Then came the war on Iraq. On March 20, 2003, the day most Iranians should have been celebrating Nowrouz, or Persian New Year, the United States started bombing Iraq. In what the U.S. government would label the "Shock and Awe" period, the United States Air Force literally paralyzed Baghdad in those early days of the war. I remember hearing about the first civilian casualty in the first few days of bombing, a Jordanian taxi driver who was in the wrong place at the wrong time. My heart sank at the impersonal bombing that would kill many civilian Iraqis in a very personal way.

In those early days, most Americans bought into the idea of war, having been sold on the idea that Saddam Hussein had an arsenal of weapons of mass destruction at his fingertips and was ready to start bombing the United States at any moment. The Bush administration had alluded to all sorts of connections to Al Qaida and the bombing of the United States by the terrorists of 9/11. Before long, the truth became evident after the infrastructure of Iraq had been completely obliterated. There were no weapons of mass destruction, and Saddam, a tyrant, but a secular tyrant, had nothing to do with Osama bin Laden. The truth was that under Saddam's rule, the fundamentalists had stayed out of Iraq. He had made sure of that.

In the United States, the anti-war protests began, and the outrage at having been lied to by their government was tangible at these demonstrations. I participated in several of them on Los Angeles and San Diego, and I saw some of the best of American culture come out to voice their displeasure. During that time, however, the Bush administration was running wild, and no one was able to stop them. Their group of forty-nine countries, who joined the ranks of what the Bush administration referred to as "the coalition of the willing," quickly dwindled in support. Only four countries from that group sent troops to Iraq.

My feeling during this time was that the bombing was simply too close to my country. After including Iran with Iraq and North Korea as part of the Axis of Evil, I felt that the Bush administration already had a plan for Iran. What is important to understand about my country is that as much as we might disagree with our own government, we will fight for our country against outside forces. The Iraq War improved the numbers of young people signing up early for their mandatory military service in Iran. I was opposed to any kind of war. I had lived through the Iran-Iraq War, which was responsible for keeping Khomeini in power after the Revolution. Iranians felt he would lead their country to the other side of that war. I had seen what the casualties of war can do to a country. The hundreds of thousands who died in the Iran-Iraq War and all those maimed and left disabled from injuries during the war were staggering.

I also knew how much occupation had hurt my country in the past. During the World War II, Iran was occupied by Russia, England, and the United States. Later, when the United Kingdom and the United States overthrew the democratic government of Iranian Prime Minister Mossadeqh, our country was led down a path that ended with the takeover of the mullahs of the Revolution in 1979. Foreign occupation and war would never be the answer to freedom for my country.

Out of the ashes of the war came the news of abuses at Abu Gharib and later Guantanamo. My own outrage at these examples made me even more certain that my silence in my political work against this Islamic Republic was the right move at that time. It was a decision I didn't take lightly, and in fact I wrestled for months with whether I should quit politics completely for that time or continue in some way.

I started looking for jobs that would have flexible schedules so I could go back to school. A friend suggested that I sell cars for a while, save enough money to go back to school, and practice my English with customers. This sounded reasonable at the time. I had no idea of what I walked into, but as fate would have it, I was a fairly decent car salesman. My monthly numbers were usually high, but my biggest fault was that I couldn't let customers pay for unnecessary add-ons to the cars they bought from me. On a couple of occasions I told my customers when the Finance Department was trying to sell them unneeded services, and on both occasions I was fired.

The time from July 2002 until July 2006 was dark in many ways. I was lonely for much of that time. On a couple of occasions, I traveled to Europe to see new students who had left Iran and were seeking political asylum there.

In those dark days I would often remember the struggles of those in my country who had come before me. I remembered the poor people of my country who were living in extreme poverty. I remembered the years that followed the overthrow of Prime Minister Mossadeqh. There is a very famous photo of him as he is being tried for treason following the coup in 1953, where Mossadeqh sits at a table, his head resting on his forearms, his eyes downcast, while those around him smile for the photo. Mossadeqh spent three years in prison, and the rest of his life under house arrest in his home in Amad Abad. Those years must have been a thousand times worse than any of mine, and because of this, I never lost sight of my goal. In my darkest moments, I remembered Mossadeqh, I remembered the students still held in Islamic regime prisons because of the work we had done for freedom in July 1999, and I put my head down and worked, knowing that eventually I would reappear and begin to build our movement again.

There were times when it would have been easy to sink into feelings of hopelessness. There were those in the Iranian community in Los Angeles who questioned me leaving Iran and my loyalty to Manouchehr and the rest who remained in Evin prison. I knew they would eventually know the truth, and that my friends still in prison in Iran all knew my position in our movement. Political prisoners who serve long sentences in Islamic regime prisons are sometimes granted temporary releases. During some of these releases, Manouchehr and others in our group were able to make contact with me to let me know that they continued to have confidence in me.

My silence finally ended as the war in Iraq was at an all-time high, the United States government refused to consider the overall displeasure its citizens felt about the war. At that time, the Bush administration still had two more years to wreak havoc on the world, and the rumblings that they had strategic plans in place to begin bombing Iran were in the media almost every day. Iranian people in Los Angeles were starting to talk about the possibility of war in Iran. What seems unbelievable is that there are many within the community who believe that a U.S. attack on Iran would be a good thing. They believed that a U.S. military strike would lead to regime change in Iran, and that anything would be better than the mullahs who currently control Iran. To this belief, I continually point out the situation in Iraq. People there are not free, and for many the situation continues to deteriorate. In 2006, the war in Iraq was continuing to escalate, and there seemed no end in sight.

I decided to plan the first Iranian anti-war protest on the anniversary of July 1999 in 2006. As one of the leaders of the student movement in Iran, I wanted to make a statement that we would not support a military strike by the United States. I invited Dr. Mehrdad Darvishpour, a well-known professor of sociology in Stockholm. I also invited Iranian poet Majid Nafisi. The turnout was small, with barely two hundred people, yet the message was more important than the quantity of people attending. The International Alliance of Iranian Students was the first to come out against a war with Iran. Our demonstration was, of course, boycotted by the Persian Mafia's media in Los Angeles, but the local media did give us some limited coverage.

The next day I was sitting in a car talking politics to Dr. Darvishpour before he left to return to Stockholm when my cell phone rang. When I answered, the voice on the other end of the line had an American accent and said he was from the Federal Bureau of Investigation and he wanted to talk to me. I couldn't imagine why the FBI would be calling me, and asked him how I could verify that he was who he said he was, to which he gave me his name and office number. He asked me where I was, so they could set up a meeting with me. At the time I was in Reseda, California, and he suggested a coffee shop on Ventura Boulevard right away. I hung up the phone in disbelief, and told Dr. Darvishpour what I had just heard. He was concerned and offered to postpone his trip back to Sweden, to which I assured him I would be okay and that he should keep his reservations.

The next day, before I went to the coffee shop, I called several friends to let them know where I would be in case anything happened to me. I came from a country where someone could go missing in a situation like this, and at that point I had no idea why the FBI wanted to meet with me. I sat waiting at The Coffee Bean in Reseda, sipping a cup of green tea. The two agents who walked in looked like any stereotypical

FBI agent from just about any American movie of the last twenty years. One was large and beefy and looked like an American football player, the other was average height and seemed to be the most senior of the two. The larger agent handed me his FBI business card and introduced himself as Special Agent Christopher Castillo from the Los Angeles office.

The conversation started aggressively from the start. Agent Castillo told me that they knew about the protest I had organized and told me he was there to warn me that I needed to be very careful about the kinds of things I was saying. I told him that I was only expressing my opinions, that I believed in democracy, and that this was my right in the United States. He interrupted me, saying, "You were just showing off for the protest, but you need to be careful. You aren't a U.S. citizen, and because of that you don't have any value here. You amount to zero in our book." I was puzzled by his words, and in all truth, I hadn't come across this sort of interrogation since leaving Islamic regime prisons. I asked him to clarify what he meant by that, and he went on, "Here we have a system, and in that system, you are nothing. You want to protest a war in Iran, and I can tell you that your country isn't our problem. Our problem is protecting American lives, and if it means killing sixty million people in Iran, we don't care. We care about saving lives here in America."

The FBI agents went on to accuse me of being a member of the Mujahadeen Khalq. They reminded me that the United States considered this a terrorist organization, of which I denied being a member. They pressed me further, saying that I knew people who were part of this organization, and while I couldn't recall specifically who I might know who had ever been part of the Mujahadeen, I couldn't understand what crime I would have committed having known someone in that group. I reminded them that the Mujahadeen was supported by the United States in Iraq, and that they were against the Islamic Republic. After that, Agent Castillo replied that I was probably just involved in politics so I could make a profit from the U.S. government. At this I became angry and told him that I had been given several opportunities to profit in the United States from my political beliefs, and mentioned Senator Brownback's offer from a few years before.

I told them that I had political asylum in the United States, but that if I was unwanted, I would leave this country. I pressed Agent Castillo as to whether this was so, to which his approach softened. He said that as someone with political asylum I had to be careful. By the end of the conversation, I was left feeling that I was being watched by the U.S. government.

Months later I would hear about the case of four Iranian brothers who were accused by Agent Christopher Castillo of being part of the Mujahadeen Khalq and ended up spending more than three years in prison following September 11. Apparently, being a member of the Mujahadeen Khalq is a favorite accusation of Special Agent Christopher Castillo's. In a lawsuit filed by the Mirmehdi brothers in 2006, they claimed that the U.S. government, through FBI Agent Christopher Castillo, had taken punitive actions against the brothers when they had refused to work as FBI informants.

## REMEMBERING AKBAR

On July 30, 2006, Akbar Mohammadi died in Evin prison. Subjected to years of torture that went far beyond what I endured, his physical health was already fragile, and after more than a week of a hunger strike his body gave out. Whether his death was of natural causes as the Islamic Republic would have us think, or whether the torturers themselves stopped his heart from beating, at the end of the day Akbar died at the hands of the Islamic Republic of Iran.

I want the world to know that there has never been a better fighter for any cause than Akbar. He was strength personified. His courage in the face of such tyranny is beyond what most of us mere mortals can conceive of. At the end, his body was no longer that of a thirty-seven-year-old man. He suffered from a loss of hearing in one of his ears, and he had major kidney problems, and internal bleeding.

Akbar's legacy in the student movement was that he came to signify torture by the Islamic Republic. I will never forget that last time when I saw Akbar Mohammadi as we were being transferred from Tohid to Evin prison. Akbar and I believed that the hard times were over for both of us, and that we would be sent to the student section of Evin to wait out the remainder of our sentences. We shook hands in the car on the way over, locking our fingers together for a short embrace before we reached our destination. We were happy at that moment, and in his lovely way, he reassured me that everything was going to be okay.

When we reached Evin prison, the guards separated us. They took Akbar to Section 209 of the prison. While the extreme torture of Tohid had ended for me, Akbar's would continue at Evin prison. Eventually he was moved with the other student prisoners, but the toll on his body was simply too high. He suffered more than any of us for his beliefs.

Before his last days at Evin prison, he had very limited time outside of prison walls. He was released on a few occasions because of his physical ailments so that he could seek medical help. During one of those releases, a book was published in the United States in Akbar's name. It was promoted via satellite that beamed into Iran, Not long after that, the Islamic authorities picked Akbar up and took him back to Evin prison.

I have often wondered why he didn't leave Iran during one of his temporary visits home. I believe Akbar must have thought he could endure for the movement.

The circumstances of Akbar's death have always been questionable. He was taken to the infirmary shortly before he died. He was continually beaten, even during the fast he was undertaking to protest his return to prison. It is believed that he was injected with a substance while in the infirmary, and shortly after that he died. The timing of Akbar's death is worth noting since it was fairly early in the first term of Ahmadinejad's presidency. Many of us felt killing Akbar was a message to the student movement from the Islamic Republic of Iran. The content of that message was written in Akbar's blood, but just as my friend's fire could never be contained, students in Iran would take his death as even more reason to continue our fight.

The events that followed were no less heartbreaking than the last several years of Akbar's life had been. The government wouldn't allow his family to bury him in Tehran, and neither would they agree to bury him in his hometown of Amol. He was later buried in a small village cemetery in Changemian. His body was badly beaten, and he was almost unrecognizable according to those who witnessed his remains before he was buried.

Manouchehr was allowed a temporary release because of his brother's death. It was during this time that the Kurdish Democratic Party of

Iran helped Manouchehr to escape Iran. He made his way through Iraq and Turkey, and eventually was flown by a military plane to a U.S. Air Force base in Germany.

I took Akbar's death very hard. I quit my job and took some time to grieve. Over the next few months, Akbar was always on my mind. I remembered the way he was, not only as a member of our group and a political activist, but as a friend. He was selfless in the way he shared whatever he had to give. When he saw suffering, poverty, or struggle among the people of Iran, it killed him. He became enraged to see the people of his country with nothing, while the clergy held all the wealth. His connection to the Persian culture and his love of social justice set him apart from most anyone I have ever known.

# CHAPTER 10

# IRANIAN POLITICS TODAY: WHERE ARE THE GROUPS OF RESISTANCE?

On a recent Huffington Post "Big News Page," I noticed a special section dedicated to Iran's news. This is a far cry from where it was when I first landed in the United States in 2000. In many ways, we have the current president of Iran, Mahmoud Ahmadinejad, to thank for this new notoriety. Admadinejad's band-standing in his outbursts against the Israeli state have helped to make him famous and Iran a subject of interest in the West. Iran's president has taken every opportunity to put out shocking statements, including seeing cosmic light over the heads of the audience at his first U.N. speech and declaring homosexuality nonexistent in Iran during a speech at Columbia University.

Iran is also an important topic in the news because of the U.S. wars with its neighbors, Iraq and Afghanistan. Americans in general know more about the region than they did a decade ago. While they still may not have details about the culture, it's almost impossible to find a U.S. city without some sort of Iranian presence—be it a Persian market or a university professor.

So now, with Iran being at the forefront, the question continually arises as to why so many in Iran can have so much discontent with the current regime, yet they still don't overthrow the government. The answer is a complex one, and in truth, there is perhaps no one answer. Those who have organized against the government of Iran have in many ways done so independently, disagreeing on so much that finding the ultimate common ground—how to take out the current Islamic regime—has taken a backseat.

Many of those who remained inside Iran faced violent ends at the hands of the Islamic Republic. Countless political prisoners were executed by the Islamic government since it took control in 1979. Many activists left Iran entirely, and from the outside lost touch with the real Iran as it evolved under the strong arm of Khomeini's government.

There continue to be groups that have been in disagreement with the current regime for many years, and continue their struggle inside and outside of Iran. The following is a list of those I consider, for better or worse, to be most important and to have either the longest run in their opposition, the best organization, or the most promising. All of them have had a presence in and around the student movement, and have been mentioned previously within the context of this work. However, addressing where they are at present is a means of suggesting how they will play a key role in Iran's future.

## PEOPLE'S MOJAHEDIN ORGANIZATION OF IRAN (MOJEHEDIN)

Camp Ashraf is the home to the People's Mojahedin Organization of Iran (Mojehedin) and is headquartered in Iraq for now, about seventy-five miles from the Iran's border. The government of Iraq is unsure what to do with the group that has been classified by many as a terrorist organization. It is estimated that the camp houses some 3,400 members. The group moved to Iraq in 1986 after having been asked to leave Paris by the French government.

The leader of the group, Masoud Rajavi, was one of the founding members of the Mojahedin and served on the Central Committee. The group started in 1965 out of extreme opposition to the Shah of Iran's government. Rajavi became a member of the Central Committee in 1966, and according to reports distinguished himself as the "ideological leader" of the Mojahedin organization. He was arrested along with many others by the Shah's SAVAK in 1971, where he spent the next eight years in prison, He was the only survivor of the Mojahedin's twelve-member Central Committee.

Following the Revolution of 1979, Rajavi's position was very strong. At that time, as an Islamic socialist organization, they were well-positioned to work with the new government of Iran. They considered themselves to be part of a movement of "Modern Islam."

It wasn't long before Ayatollah Khomeini turned on the Mojahedin, accusing them of having "the Western plague" because of their progressive ideas. Meeting places of Mojahedin members were attacked by Ansar-e Hezbollah, and hundreds of members were killed between 1979 and 1981. In response, the Mojehedin organized a large demonstration against the Islamic Republic in June 1981.

Abolhassan Banisadr had been elected as the first president of the Islamic Republic of Iran. Masoud Rajavi and Banisadr formed a close alliance during that time. When Banisadr and Ayatollah Khomeini had a falling out over support for the Hezbollah in Lebanon, Khomeini actively wanted Banisadr out of his position.

Banisadr also disagreed with the war with Iraq and wanted to find a resolution to the war early on—something Ayatollah Khomeini wasn't open to, as the war was helping cement the clergy's power within the country. Khomeini instigated the impeachment of Banisadr, who went into hiding before fleeing Iran and escaping to Paris with Masoud Rajavi in tow.

While the leader of the Mojehedin and Banisadr forged a close friendship during their initial time in Paris, going so far as to begin to design a new government for Iran from outside the country, in time they experienced friction between them. Rajavi wanted to go to Iraq to be closer to Iran and build the Mojehedin there. Banisadr rejected this idea, believing that going to a country that was waging war on Iran would send the wrong message to the citizens of Iran.

Rajavi cut his ties with Banisadr and moved to Iraq, where he attempted to make peace with Saddam Hussein. This lost support for the Mojehedin inside Iran, as the cost of war was so great in human life for our country. Many who had supported them in the past could no longer get behind the Mojahedin once they were in Iraq.

Once in Iraq, the Mojehedin became more heavily military-based. While they were inside Iran, members were made up of more students. Still, the Mojehedin has been heavily supported financially by its members and by Arab countries that favor a change in the Iranian government.

In the past, the Mojehedin believed that Iran should be an Islamic democratic republic. In recent years they have shifted a bit to promote a more secular government in Iran that would support a democratic republic. The group has had huge sacrifice in human life at the hands of the Islamic Republic, and the members who still live inside Iran cannot show outward support for the Mojahedin.

As an organization, they are extremely well organized, and because of strong financial backing, they have the ability to grow their group. I believe that the one area in which the Mojehedin fall short is that while in theory they support a democratic way of life inside Iran, their organization isn't run in a democratic way. They believe that they are the only organization capable of overthrowing the Islamic Republic, and this has caused a kind of distance from other groups with similar interests.

My view of the Mojehedin is that they have several issues to overcome in order to work toward change in Iran. The first is that the organization still holds to an ideology that includes Islam. I believe that if they truly are interested in democracy, they must reexamine their Islamic ideology. Second, they need to accept other groups working toward the same goals as part of the opposition of the Islamic Republic of Iran. For the Mojehedin to have an active role in establishing democracy in Iran, they must be willing to do this. Additionally, as with many outside of Iran, the Mojehedin need to understand that the Iran they left twenty-five or thirty years ago is a far different place today. Forming alliances with other groups will help bridge those changes and make all the groups stronger.

The current state of Camp Ashraf is unclear. Iran would like Iraq to return the members of Mojehedin to Iran. Iraq no longer wants Camp Ashraf on its soil. My belief is that the United States will use Camp Ashraf as a bargaining chip in negotiations with Iran. What I mean by this is not that the United States will turn the inhabitants of Camp Ashraf over to Iran, but that they will leverage the removal in a way that will benefit Iran, Iraq, and the United States and be acceptable to members of Mojehedin.

# THE LEFTISTS AND SOCIALISTS

The Leftist movement in Iran goes back to the days of Reza Shah, the father of the deposed Shah from 1979. The Communist Party of the day was instrumental in founding the Union of Oil Workers in 1925. By 1929, Reza Shah passed a bill through the Majlis to ban communist activities, forcing Iranian communists underground—something they would grow accustomed to over time. One of the early leaders of leftists in Iran, Dr. Taghi Arani, and what became known as The Group of 53, were arrested because of their political activities. After two years in Iranian prison, Dr. Arani's case was finally heard in front of a court. At his trial, Dr. Arani was his own defense. He spent six hours in front of the court, and he set out to convince the court of the merits of Marxism. Dr. Arani later died in prison.

With Dr. Arani's passing, however, leftist ideology was not gone from Iran, and in fact his era of the movement gave birth to the Hazb Tudeh, one of the best known communist parties of Iran. During the twentieth century, while the party spoke of lofty ideas of social justice, freedom, social progress, and the ideas of scientific socialism, they were heavily connected to Soviet Russia. Their stance grew in intensity against nationalism and imperialism.

As the Tudeh party evolved, there were issues that caused tensions with other left groups. The Tudeh members believed they should be the only communist group within Iran, and their ties to the Soviets became a priority. During Mossadeqh's time, they believed that Iran's oil should be nationalized in the southern part of the country, but that the northern areas where the oil industry existed should be controlled by the Soviets. In 1953, the Tudeh party took orders from the Soviet Union in their response to the overthrow of Iran's prime minister. While it might be strong to say that the Tudeh Party sided with the United States in the coup that overthrew Mossadeqh, they did little to dissuade it and they certainly didn't stand behind Mossadeqh. They were opposed to a democratic Iran, and in favor of Soviet Russia reaping some of the profits of the Iranian oil industry. There are few groups in Iran who have less support from masses of Iranian people than the Tudeh. Even other leftist groups have a saying in Farsi that is basically translated as "Tudeh=Traitor."

Over time, members of the Tudeh party started branching out into their own groups. One such group was founded in 1964, called the Organization of the Iranian People's Fedayee Guerrillas (Fedayeen). The Fedayeen were considered "new communists" and they consisted of two factions, one that advocated armed struggle and was led by Masoud Ahmadzadeh, formerly of the National Front, and Amir Parvis Pouyan, and the other led by Bizhan Jazani. In the years before the Islamic Revolution, the Fedayeen was a target for extreme persecution by the monarchist government of the Shah of Iran. More than any other group, they were victims of torture, imprisonment, and executions.

By 1978, the Fedayeen organization started to grow in numbers. Attracted to the Fedayeen's ideology, the number of students within the group grew. By that time, both Masoud Ahmadzadeh and Bizhan Jazani had been killed by the Shah's government. Strongly opposed to the government of the Shah, in the weeks just before the Revolution of 1979, the Fedayeen had a demonstration at Tehran University that included some fifty thousand protestors.

After the Revolution, the Fedayeen officially split into two different organizations. The first group included members of the followers of Ahmadzadeh, and they called themselves Charik Fedayee Aghliat. The Aghliat side of the Fedayeen was a minority, and while they welcomed the overthrow of the Shah's government, they saw the Islamic ideology of Khomeini as more of a means to an end than as a long-term solution. They paid dearly for this stance and the loss of their members was staggering. The other organization was the Cherik Fedayee Aksariat, the organization that had the majority of members, and was made up of the followers of Jazani. The Aksariat members of the Fedayeen supported the Islamic government proposed by Khomeini during the Revolution. Later, they too would reject the Islamic Republic's government.

Once the government of Iran was firmly under Khomeini's rule, the cooperation that had been promised before the Revolution changed, and leftist groups, just as had happened to the Mujahadeen, were out of favor. Many of those who were part of both the Aksariat and the Aghliat branches of the Fedayeen left Iran. Of the Aksariat members still left in Iran in 1997, some became supporters of the reformist era of Khatami's administration. Many of the Aghliat group migrated to

Europe and adopted a more social democratic approach, though some stayed within the communist beliefs.

As I have mentioned, another group that continues today is the Worker-Communist Party of Iran. They continue to push for a revolutionary overthrow of the Islamic Republic, and a new socialist republic put in its place. Current day Aghliats would like to see a secular government in Iran based on social democracy, and while this is also true of the Aksariats outside Iran, Aksariats have evolved in their social democratic ideology. Additionally, there has always been an outstanding question among many other groups—the Aghliats and Mujahadeen in particular—about the possible cooperation between Aksariats and the Islamic regime. There are those who believe that the Aksariats formed an alliance with the Islamic regime that helped in attacking members of other groups. Members of the Tudeh party are fairly few in number, and inside Iran they live in secret. Those still left have little or no contact with other Tudeh members, so as a group they have little strength. The Tudeh in general have less support from other groups than most because of their past.

There also exist other groups who are considered communist within Iranian politics both inside and outside the country. Two such groups are in Europe: The Etehad Jomhourikhahan and Jomhourikhahan Democt Va Laik.

The Etehad Jomhourikhahan doesn't identify as communist, but the common belief is that many of their members are actually communists and supporters of the Reformist movement. Additionally, the Etehad Jomhourikhahan doesn't necessarily believe in getting rid of the current regime in the Islamic Republic of Iran. Instead, members believe in reforming the government that is currently in place. They are against the monarchy and want a focus on a socialist government in Iran that would be similar to that of Scandinavian countries.

The Jomhourikhahan Democt Va Laik are secular and not all members are communist. They are supportive of a secular democracy and believe in a complete change in the regime that does not include a return to the monarchy.

In general, as I have stated, the left movement isn't united, and for this reason they lack a collective power. What is baffling is that most of them have the ultimate goal of unseating the Islamic Republic, and many have very similar beliefs in what should be put in its place. Still, the infighting between groups has kept Iranian socialists from having a cohesive message that allows them to make any real impact. This isn't to say that they have no place in the current movement in Iran; however, there is a need for these groups, and all others, to put aside their differences and band together for a common goal.

## THE MONARCHISTS

There's no way to wrap any of the political groups of Iran into a nice neat package, and that is even true of the monarchists. In a simplistic way, I could say that they are all followers of the former monarchy, and that their ideological leader is Mohammed Reza Shah's heir, Reza Pahlavi. But in truth, the Monarchist movement today is as complex as any of the other movements.

Today in Iran it is still illegal to be a member of the Monarchist Party. The idea of the Shah of Iran being part of a memory or what some older citizens would consider "the good old days" still exists today. Those who believe it inside the country, however, do so in secret. They often believe that a democracy would be possible, but with a monarchist at the head—much as is practiced today in Sweden, The Netherlands, the United Kingdom, and Japan.

It is easy to rewrite history to seem monumentally better than the current situation. As I have said, in truth, the Shah was a better choice for Iran than the Islamic Republic has been, but in my opinion, not the best choice. During the years of monarchy, just as in the years since, the general populous of our country has been in search of freedom and democracy.

Outside of Iran, the monarchist population has been very financially successful. Many who left either just before the Revolution or shortly thereafter were able to take much of their wealth with them to make a start outside of Iran. Others, who weren't as fortunate to have immigrated with money, came to Western countries where some of them became very successful.

Their leader, Reza Pahlavi, is a fairly humble man, though his lineage is considered royalty. While some of his followers have referred to him as "His Imperial Majesty Reza Shah II," he prefers to be called simply "Reza Pahlavi" or "the former crown prince." Reza Pahlavi has said that he believes in democracy, and he has spent much of his life living in the United States. His idea is that first the government of Iran must change, and once the country is free, the people of Iran should decide if they want to restore the Peacock Throne of the Pahlavi dynasty.

Reza Pahlavi has said that he supports a separation of government and religion, and encourages nonviolent civil disobedience.

Of the monarchists outside of Iran, there is a small percentage who are not followers of Reza Pahlavi. This group believes that Pahlavi should claim his role as king of Iran. They don't believe he should wait for a change in government, but instead should be leading regime change in Iran as the "official" king. Their foundational belief, coming from the days of the Shah, is that the rule of Iran should follow a model of "God, King, and Nation," and requires more from a future king than what Reza Pahlavi has proposed so far. Many of the remaining monarchists believe in large part in a government similar to Sweden and the UK, where Reza Pahlavi would act as a royal figurehead when returned to the throne.

I believe that the followers of the monarchy have evolved over the last thirty years and are quite different from the followers of the Shah prior to the Revolution. Many of those who were loyal to the Shah believed in the absolute power of the royal leader. But just as the members of the left have evolved from a strict communist ideology to more social democratic leanings, so have many monarchists embraced an idea of Reza Pahlavi serving as a figure head instead of ruling as king. Additionally, there are fewer of the old monarchists today, as they have aged, and now their children, who have been raised outside of the country, have far different political views than their parents. These descendants of the monarchists are key to the future of Iran from the perspective that they have been raised with the concept of the separation of church and state, and they are secular.

In fact, all of the monarchists are important for the future of Iran because of their secular viewpoint, a desire for democracy, and their cultural ties to Iran. To judge all monarchists based on my experience with those who have taken over the Los Angeles Iranian media is unfair. While old Iranian money does continue to control much of the community, there are those who don't agree with their approach, even in southern California. Many Iranians outside the mainstream circles in southern California do not agree with the monopoly on Iranian media that exists today. They have witnessed the way in which the power-yielding monarchists in Los Angeles caused political rifts within our own student group, and they have taken issue with the individuals who were instrumental in doing so.

Still, there needs to be some reform to the idea that all was perfect before the Revolution. Those who left after the mullahs took over the country must understand that the system wasn't working for the Revolution to have occurred. Iranians inside the country, particularly the younger generation, are more politically sophisticated. They have been exposed to the outside world because of technology, and they are ready for a whole new kind of government in Iran.

Where the monarchists may find challenge is in their ideological leader's lack of a track record in leading a country. Reza Pahlavi was quite young when he left Iran, and while he has been educated in the United States and Europe, he has not had the experience of leading anything as large as an entire country. For him to be anything more than a figurehead would require proof that he can lead. To go up against the Islamic Republic will take more than popularity and charisma. It will take political savvy that is able to seize every opportunity to take Iran into the future. Whether Reza Pahlavi has that kind of savvy remains to be seen.

## THE NATIONAL FRONT

The National Front was founded in the late 1940s by Mohammed Mossadeqh. From its inception, it was never really a party per se, but represented a joining of forces for several groups, including the Iran Party, the Toilers Party, the National Party, and the Tehran Association of Bazaar Trade and Craft Guilds. Those who belonged to the first National Front were generally nationalists who believed in social democracy.

The National Front was leading the opposition to European control of Iran's natural resources during Mossadeqh's time. With the passing of the Oil Nationalization Act by the Iranian Parliament in 1951, the wheels were set in motion to overthrow the government of Mohammed Mossadeqh. Following the coup d'état in 1953, the National Front was outlawed in Iran. In response to this, several members of the National

Front established an underground National Resistance Movement. By 1960, the Second National Front was born and consisted of such well-known leaders as Karim Sanjabi, Mehdi Bazargan, Allahyar Saleh, Shapour Bakhtiar, and Dariush Forouhar. The Second National Front believed in Mossedeqh as their leader. They also wanted to reestablish the government that had come out of the Constitutional Revolution. At that time, the group had a good chance; however, infighting among the highest ranks led the National Front to again lose focus.

In my mind, the most important factor surrounding the National Front of the past and going forward all the way up until today is that they are considered the followers of Mossadeqh. That being said, they carry an enormous responsibility of continuing on in his absence. Mossadeqh set the bar very high, and those who came after him have a very difficult act to follow.

Perhaps one of the most distinct examples of National Front leadership facing challenges in modern day Iran would come some twelve years after Mossadeqh's death, just a matter of days before the Islamic Revolution. In January 1979, the Shah of Iran appointed Shapur Bakhtiar, a National Front member, as the prime minister of Iran. His rule would last only thirty-six days, but in that time he managed to rid Iran of the violent SAVAK secret police that had terrorized the country under the Shah's command.

When Bakhtiar accepted the position of prime minister, he held a deep conviction that Iran was in grave danger should the government be turned over the Khomeini. He believed that the Mashrutiyyat, the Iranian Constitution that had been won in the revolution between 1905 and 1911 and had established a parliamentary system in Iran, would be lost should the mullahs take control of the government. History would show that in this point, Bakhtiar was right.

At that time, many within the National Front were so eager to see the fall of the Shah that they sided with the likes of Ayahollah Khomeini and supported the Revolution. Others in the National Front, like Karim Sanjabi, aligned themselves with Khomeini prior to the Revolution. Acting as a representative of the National Front, Sanjabi traveled to Paris while Khomeeini was still in exile there and signed an agreement with him that included democracy as part of the alliance between the Islamic ideology and the overthrow of the Shah. Once the Shah had been deposed, however, Khomeini went back on his word, and refused the wording that had gone into the agreement between the two sides.

This would be the first of many times the Islamic Republic of Iran did not keep their word to the leaders of the National Front. While Khomeini and his cronies had promised collaboration with members of the National Front prior to the Revolution, in the end, these same promises held no more weight than the ones that had been made to the Iranian leftists or the Mojahadeen. By 1980, Khomeini was stating in speeches that the National Front and Mossadeqh were not Muslims.

This would be the beginning of the end of any collaboration between Khomeini's theocrats and the National Front. In June 1981, the Islamic Republic's parliament approved the use of the Islamic law of Qisas within the new government. In the Quran, the law of Qisas is the equivalent to the biblical "eye for an eye" and is sometimes called the law of retribution or blood revenge. The National Front began staging a demonstration that was to take place in Tehran on June 15, 1981. They went on a campaign to call the people of Iran out into the streets, distributing some four million leaflets.

Just before the demonstration was to begin, Ayatollah Khomeini gave a radio address in which he stated that anyone participating in the protest was inviting an uprising and part of an insurrection. In his speech, he stated, "The National Front is condemned as of today," and threatened its leaders with execution should they not repent immediately.

By 1982, the National Front was abolished inside Iran and many of its leaders had left the country. Today in Iran a small group of members of the National Front still exists, though most of them are aging, with few from the younger generation continuing the movement inside Iran. Outside of Iran there are National Front members all over the world.

The problem that exists within the organization today is its lack of a centralized group of leaders. Most members of the National Front are spread out all over the world, with little contact among them. While several groups have set up Web sites and have attempted to establish a presence, their lack of unification has cost the movement.

The importance of the National Front is that they continue to carry on the legacy of Mossadeqh. They are his living representatives, and I believe they must continue. To do that, there needs to be a way of uniting members and creating reform that will involve the younger generation, including women. The National Front needs to establish a way of connecting members across geographical locations and generations. Mossadeqh has a captive audience in the youth both inside and outside of Iran. This is particularly powerful in that Mossadeqh believed in the new generations of Iran leading the way toward progress for the country. Additionally, Mossadeqh saw the National Front not as a single organization, but instead as a "front" that included several likeminded groups. Although the National Front never succeeded in transforming Iran, Mossadeqh's dreams live on.

## WOMEN'S AND LABOR MOVEMENTS

The last two activist groups I want to mention are the Women's Movement and the Labor Movement in Iran. Women in Iran still suffer at the hands of the Islamic Republic, and their movement has become a very strong voice of opposition within the country in recent years.

In 2003, Shirin Ebadi became the first Iranian to be awarded the Nobel Peace Prize for her work for democracy and human rights in Iran. She has focused much of her work around women's issues in Iran. She is also the first Muslim woman to win the award. Ebadi's work both before and after winning the Nobel Peace Prize has given strength to women's causes in Iran.

Still, in Iran, women hold half the value legally as do their male counterparts. In the court of law, two women have the value of one man. Yet well over half the students in universities in Iran today are female, and this is a trend that is going to continue. These women's voices have become stronger and the government is faced with their activism on an ongoing basis.

The Labor Party in Iran has become more active in the last several years. Their movement is important to the workers in Iran because of the current economic challenges facing the country. As this group continues its fight for workers rights, and as they join with other groups, their strength will increase.

## STUDENT MOVEMENT

Today, the strongest movement and catalyst for change inside Iran lies with the student organizations. I believe that the work our group did in 1999, and the events that led up to the attacks on the dormitories, helped open the door to the strength that we are now seeing within the student movement inside Iran. At no time was this more evident than following the 2009 reelection of Mahmoud Ahmadinejad.

What began with signs asking, "Where Is My Vote?" has quickly evolved into chants that a decade ago we could only say behind closed doors. In 2009, demonstrators wearing green sashes and ribbons were chanting slogans like, "We will fight, we will die, we will get our country back!" and "Death to Khamanei."

This didn't happen overnight. What we began in 1999 grew over the last ten years. In December 2006, during a visit by President Ahmadenejad, students of Amir Kabir University in Tehran held up signs with the words "Fascist President" and "Death to the Dictator." As their chants escalated, students burned photos of Ahmadenejad while the president looked shocked and unsure how to respond. Reports said that he encouraged his supporters to begin with religious chanting, even joining in himself with slogans hailing Ahmadenejad.

What is encouraging to me about this show of protest is that I believe it is evidence of the evolution of the movement. Before July 1999, even talking amongst friends about opposition to the government was risky behavior. Back then, having someone in your family be imprisoned for political activity was very damaging, and to some degree it still is, yet for the older generations there is respect for the youth who are willing to make sacrifices for their beliefs. Yet, the price is very high. Islamic regime prisons have no better of a record on human rights violations than they did before, and students who voice their opposition must go into hiding to keep from being imprisoned and tortured. Since the elections of 2009, the human rights issues have escalated considerably, and the stories coming out of Iran are more disturbing than ever.

Today there are four distinct parts to the student movement in Iran. The first, the Daftar-e-Tahkim-e-Vahdat, continues to be very active in Iran, but has had a major transformation in the past ten years. The newer generation of the Daftar-e-Tahkim-e-Vahdat is divided into one part that still followings the Islamic Republic's hard line, and the other that is in opposition to the theocrats of the government. The side of the group that challenges the government is not as religious as its earlier members. After having been followers of President Mohammed

Khatami and let down by the lack of reform that he was actually able to produce, members have become more secular in their approach.

The second group of students who are making headlines represent the left movement. This group has been particularly active over the last several years, and via the technology of the Internet has made contact with groups outside of Iran. While this group opposes the fundamentalism of the Islamic Republic, they also are in opposition to U.S. policy when it comes to any sort of bombing of Iran that was part of the Bush administration's agenda. Believing that the Reformist movement failed, they tend to lean more toward a radical idea of overthrowing the government. Many of those who were part of our group or other secular groups in 1999 became part of the more radical left in Iran. This idea of leftism is different from the Communist movement of thirty years ago. They hold great value for the Iranian culture, and there is a hint of movement toward democracy in their idea as well. However, the new left is against globalization and strongly opposed to war.

The third group of students in Iran are the secular democrats. They believe in maintaining the cultural identity of Iran, and that studying the historical context of the political past holds that answers to Iran's current issues with the Islamic Republic. They believe in integrating some Western ideology into Iranian culture, particularly democracy, development, technology, and freedom. This group is made up of both social and liberal democrats, and many are also followers of Mossadeqh.

This third group isn't currently organized, but instead supports both the Daftar-e-Tahkim-e-Vahdat students as well as the leftist students. Just as the first two groups support opposition to the Islamic Republic and a separation of religion and government, so too do the secular democrats. What is different among the groups of today compared to the movement in 1999 is that there doesn't seem to be the same kinds of infighting between them. Their numbers are large and they can achieve great power when organized. They have taken a grassroots approach in which small groups in various locations take to the streets and chant from the rooftops at night.

The last student group that still exists today is the Basij Daneshjooyi. They are part of the Islamic Republic and are the student branch of the Sepah Pasdaran. They follow the Supreme Leader Ali Khamanei, and they exist in the university to control the other students. The Basij Daneshjooyi has offices in virtually every university in Iran, and they have direct communication within the government agencies of the Islamic Republic. Members of Basij Daneshjooyi are exempt from taking university entrance exams.

In the end, the most important move the opposition groups could make is to come together for the common goal of removing the Islamic regime. This isn't to say that they will form one group. They would continue separately, as each of them serves to balance the others out. What they have in common is a desire to remove the current Islamic government. They come from the same roots, though they are cultural differences depending on when and if they left the country, and they generally agree that a secular, democratic government is the best answer for Iran.

# CHAPTER 11

# THE GREEN MOVEMENT AND A GIRL NAMED NEDA

It's been ten years now since July 1999 and the attack on the dorms at Tehran University. A decade later, a fraudulent election gave the presidential seat once again to Khamanei's pick, Mahmoud Ahmadenejad. I believe Khamanei miscalculated how the citizens of Iran would respond. People were outraged. They participated in the elections, voting for the other candidates, most notably the favorite, Mir-Hossein Mousavi, and not far behind, Mehdi Karroubi. The morning following the elections the government announced a landslide victory for the incumbent, Mahmoud Ahmadenejad.

What followed was weeks of protest inside Iran. Unlike July 1999, the protesters were not confined to the youth, but consisted of young, old, educated, working class, men, women—the full gambit of Iranian society. The marches were peaceful in nature and were met with extreme violence by the Islamic Republic of Iran.

On June 20, 2009, the killing of an innocent young woman who came out to support the protesters sparked global outrage. Her name was Neda Agha Soltan, and her death was literally captured on a cell phone camera and broadcast around the world via Facebook, Twitter, and You Tube. She was a twenty-six-year-old music student who was accompanied by one of her professors. The initial belief was that she was shot from a rooftop by one of the Basiji gunmen who aimed directly for her heart. It has since come out that the gunman was more likely there on the street level. A doctor who happened to be passing by tried to stop the bleeding as the camera captured the last moments of her life. He was later interviewed by the BBC and said that a Basiji member close by started screaming shortly after the shooting that he hadn't meant to kill her. What speaks to the peaceful nature of the protesters during that time is how the onlookers handled what was essentially a confession to the shooting of Neda. Instead of taking revenge or turning him over to authorities who would most certainly have released him within hours, they took his identification and let him go.

What struck me most the first time I watched the video was that Neda looked out of the corner of her eyes in disbelief. She was shocked that she had been hit, and those around her screamed in horror as her young life slipped away. The image of her lying there on the corner of Khosravi and Salehi, her young face first clear and then slowly becoming covered in blood, is forever etched in the minds of anyone who sees the video. Within hours, the image was pouring out over online media outlets, and eventually shown by CNN and other media.

What Neda represented to the world was everything that was wrong with the elections. More than that, it was a blatant show of how far the Islamic regime was willing to go to suppress its people. Neda's death on camera showed the world in no uncertain terms how the regime deals with anyone who questions their theocratic rule. It was no longer a matter of people like me who suffered in secret prisons that the Islamic regime could say never existed. How they dealt with Neda was right there, out in the open, for the world to see.

In the days that followed, Neda's family wasn't allowed to give their daughter a proper funeral. Mosques were instructed by the government that they couldn't have memorial services in her honor. Finally, when people put flowers on the spot where Neda was killed, the government sent out a garbage truck that dumped trash on top of the makeshift memorial spot. They would later try to pin the murder of Neda on the "opposition" and even go so far as to accuse the United States of collaborating with protesters to kill Neda. The doctor who had tried to save her life, Dr. Arash Hejazi, was forced to flee from Iran back to the UK where he has residence.

In truth, Neda's end was at least quicker than the deaths of many others over the next several weeks. On the Friday before her death,

Khamenei made his first public appearance since the elections. In his address at Friday prayers, he expressed his support for Ahmadenejad and warned of violence against the protesters should the demonstrations continue. Neda's death was only the beginning of Khamenei making good on his promise. That same day we heard via Tweets and Facebook postings that some ten thousand mercenaries landed at Tehran International Airport. They were said to have been imported from places like Lebanon and Palestine—places that feel a certain indebtedness to the Islamic Republic of Iran for all its financial support. Finding Iranians willing to kill other Iranians can have its challenges.

Over the next several weeks, the word from Iran of violence used against protesters was beyond disturbing. People were pulled from their houses in the middle of the night, beaten in the streets, thrown from bridges, and arrested en masse. There were reports of prisons being so overcrowded that prisoners filled the hallways of the jails and had to sleep in shifts. We heard that the regime had started using schoolhouses and even football fields to house the political prisoners.

Based on the stories that came across the wires via Twitter and Facebook, the Islamic Republic has honed its torture methods to new heights of cruelty. We heard reports of rape of both female and male political prisoners.

As always, the numbers of casualties didn't add up. What the regime claims can never really be counted on, so families had to rely on social network sites and Web sites devoted to Iran's dead and detained to find news about loved ones. Mothers and grandmothers began holding vigils outside Evin prison, awaiting some small bit of news about their children.

For those who got the worst of news, that their loved ones had been killed, they were charged the added insult of a bullet tax by the Islamic Republic—a three thousand dollar fee for the return of your loved one's body—essentially the cost of killing them. This tax became popular in the days following the Islamic Revolution for anyone suspected of being against the new regime and literally was used to pay for the bullets exhausted in their killing.

And yet, through it all, the protests continued. Some reports stated that police forces were less likely to be as brutal as the Basiji thugs, and some even came over to the side of the protesters. By day, people came out into the streets all over Iran. Numbers have been estimated at varying times in the millions. Night after night the voices would begin from the rooftops, a call and response of the demonstrators chanting "Allaho Akbar" or "God is great." The choice of this chant is brilliant in its calling upon the same God as the Islamic Republic touts in its theocratic dictatorship. It shows a strategic position by the young opposition in their fight against the regime. The chant sends a message of peace and nonviolence, but protest nonetheless.

Outside of Iran, support for the demonstrations began almost immediately. In the Bay Area of the United States, we had our first protest on Saturday, June 13, 2009. What started as a small group gradually grew. Members of our group in London held daily protests in front of the embassy of the Islamic Republic of Iran over the next several weeks. Groups came together as we never had before, staging global days of action in support of the people of Iran.

For at least a couple of weeks, Iran had the attention of the global news media and twenty-four hour continuous coverage on CNN. Non-Iranians got a sense of what was happening in Iran. For the first time, I believe, people understood the extent to which Iranian citizens rejected the regime. Often Americans would say to me that they understood, having lived through the 2000 elections between George W. Bush and Al Gore. I appreciated the attempt at empathy, but had to respectfully disagree with the comparison. While there were likely irregularities in the 2000 U.S. presidential election, a more than 60 percent landslide victory by Ahmadinejad is not quite the same thing. The likelihood of U.S. citizens being imprisoned, tortured, or killed for siding with Al Gore would never cross most Americans' minds. People in Iran were fighting for their lives, and their cries of "Where is My Vote?" meant more than questioning the outcome of the elections. What they were really asking was, "Where is My Freedom?" and "Where is My Democracy?" Their protests were a response to three decades of repression by a theocratic dictatorship. It was a question of democracy and basic human rights for the people of Iran. At no time did Americans understand more the difference between a theocracy and a democracy.

As far as how the Obama administration has reacted, they have taken a fairly "hands-off" approach. While most Iranians would agree that foreign intervention in the form of military action is not welcome,

I believe support for human rights in Iran has been somewhat lacking. Obama made campaign promises to have dialogue with the government of Iran, and the election results have put him between a rock and a hard place. If he condemns the results, he is meddling and loses the chance to negotiate with them. If he says nothing, he essentially seems to be in agreement with them.

On June 27, 2009, I posted the following open letter to President Barack Obama on my blog and on various Web sites. I also sent the letter directly to the White House. As of this writing, I have yet to receive an answer.

## LETTER TO PRESIDENT BARACK OBAMA

Dear President Obama,

In just a few days we will mark the tenth anniversary of the student uprisings in Iran that cracked the door open for the protests we are seeing today in response to the June 12, 2009, elections in Iran. I was part of that student movement and one of the organizers of the protests that followed violent dormitory attacks at Tehran University in July 1999. I spent several months in Islamic regime prisons before I was released and fled the country.

Over the last several weeks I have spent many hours meeting with Iranians here in the United States and also abroad. I have had phone calls with many others who are still in Iran. The question we have all been asking one another repeatedly is, "Where is Obama now?"

I followed your campaign and election, and though I'm not a U.S. citizen, as the founder of an international student organization, Global Student Alliance, I endorsed your run for the presidency. What was most appealing to me, and many like me, is that you took a stand on human rights. As you must know, human rights in Iran do not exist under the theocratic rule of the last thirty years. This isn't to say that Iran's record prior to the Revolution of 1979 was without a need for vast improvement, but nothing can compare to the barbaric treatment of Iran's citizens under the Islamic Republic's rule.

The protesters, who are at this very moment disappearing from their homes at an alarming rate, face a terror that is unfathomable. I have lived a version of what they are going through, and I can tell you firsthand that those of us who have been tortured in Islamic regime prisons will live the rest of our lives with the physical and mental scars we incurred at the hands of our torturers. Those being arrested at this time are being used as examples, and they face the most vicious treatment.

As ugly as it is, I feel as someone who lived through this that I must give you a view of what current prisoners face. It is likely that the capture will include a fairly violent beating before prisoners have been taken into the jail. Next the questioning will begin. Prisoners will be interrogated night and day, and many will lose touch with time, not even knowing how many days have passed.

The torturers will likely use one of their most common torture methods, beating the bottoms of prisoners' feet with some a plastic cord. When I first heard about this sort of torture before I experienced it, I couldn't imagine that hitting the bottoms of the feet could cause such pain. In reality, there are so many nerve ending in the feet that after the first couple of blows, the pain is no longer centralized in the feet but goes all over the body. They will question the prisoners between blows, asking for names of others who worked against Islam. They will sit on their backs as they continue beating their feet. After each session, they will take the victims outside where they will be forced to jump on their throbbing, bloody feet for twenty minutes or more. This is done so that blood comes back into the feet and the healing begins. The torturers believe that as the body begins to regenerate, it ensures that the next beatings will be even more painful than the last.

The torture rooms are often intentionally kept dark and along the top of the walls they will have a large metal pipe that runs the length of the ceiling and is sturdy enough to hold the weight of the prisoner. This was where they practice a torture method called ghapani. The victim puts one arm over his or her shoulder, reaches around and grabs the other wrist from the waist. The wrists are then secured, either with a rope or handcuffs, and the victim is hung from the ceiling by the wrists. The pain is excruciating. There are no words to describe it.

Between these beatings, prisoners will be placed in solitary confinement to await their next interrogation. The cells are usually nothing more than small closets with a single light bulb hanging from the ceiling that burns twenty-four hours a day. A favorite means of psychological torture is to make prisoners watch the torture sessions of their friends' and family. I recall a brother and sister who were in Tohid prison with me (a prison that has since been closed and made into a museum), and the brother was forced to watch as his sister was repeatedly raped. I was in jail with two close friends, Manouchehr and Akbar Mohammadi. The interrogators would often have us watch each other being tortured. Akbar died in Evin prison in 2006. In the end, I lost many friends who were seeking nonviolence and a secular, democratic Iran at hands of Iran's prison system.

As gruesome as the images I have just described are, I believe a president who believes in protecting human rights must have an understanding of what is at stake, and for this reason I have shared my experiences.

Over the last few weeks I've been concerned by your reaction to the happenings in Iran. In all honesty, my sense is that you don't have very strong advisors on Iran, or that those you do have are part of a political agenda that you may not completely grasp. I mean no disrespect by this, Mr. President, but I ask that you take a look at a few of the actions that in my mind, and in the minds of many Iranians, seems lacking focus or understanding about the current situation in Iran.

**1. Letter to Ayatollah Ali Khamenei:** Many in the Iranian community were shocked that an American president would send a letter to the Supreme Leader in the weeks preceding the election. While the content of the letter is still unclear, the message it sent to our community was that it didn't matter who won, the United States would work with him. Given the outcome of the elections and the obvious fraud that took place, it would seem that the regime was given a carte blanche go-ahead to do whatever they wanted in the election, and that the United States would bless their actions. I hope this wasn't the actual message, but surely, President Obama, you must admit that this was strategically the wrong message to send to the citizens of Iran who face the Basiji thugs in the streets of Iran in the name of freedom and democracy.

**2. Invitation of Islamic Republic of Iran Diplomats to U.S. Embassy Fourth of July Parties:** Several weeks, back a cable went out to all U.S. embassies and consulates saying the U.S. diplomats could invite their counterparts from the Islamic Republic of Iran to their Fourth of July celebrations. The invitations have since been retracted—in and of itself an Iranian cultural faux pas that is considered rude at best. The real issue here, Mr. President, is how could anyone have advised you that inviting the Islamic Republic of Iran to a celebration of Independence Day in the United States was a good idea? This is a fundamentalist regime that has no respect for human rights or independence of any kind. The message that these invitations sent to the Iranian people is that the United States accepts the regime and all its cruelty.

**3. U.S. President's Reaction to Khamenei's June 19 Declaration:** During Friday prayers on June 19, 2009, Supreme Leader Ali Khamenei issued a warning to peaceful protesters that they would not be tolerated. This warning was, in truth, a death sentence to protesters. It gave Basiji thugs the go-ahead to shoot protesters at will and take prisoners based on little or no evidence. Mr. President, you must have known what this proclamation meant to human rights in Iran, yet your reaction was tepid at best. You issued a statement that you were "very concerned," while reporters had to literally pull details out of your spokesman, Robert Gibb, who finally conceded that you "condemned the violence" used against protesters.

Mr. President, people are being flung off of bridges, shot with assault rifles from rooftops, and beaten with clubs and axes until their bones are broken and they are bleeding in the streets. The injured are being taken from hospitals and put in prisons, and Basijis are pulling people from their homes in the middle of the night to be taken in for hours of questioning and torture. Thousands of innocent people who are starved for democracy and freedom are sitting in prisons, unsure of their futures, unsure if they will live another day. They are young, old, male, female, upper, middle and working class, educated, uneducated, and illiterate. They are professors, doctors, bazaaris, and laborers. The cruelty of the regime of the Islamic Republic of Iran cares not at all for their background, but rules with equality when it comes to its barbaric acts against its citizens.

President Obama, please take a moment to consider the following:

1. For the last eight years, the U.S. president repeatedly said he supported the people of Iran, but behind that support was an unspoken threat of military violence. He grouped our country as part of the "Axis of Evil" to justify veiled threats that "all options were on the table." I did not support military action against my country then, and I still don't today. In July 2006, I was the first Iranian to organize an anti-war against Iran rally. But three years later, some sort of protection must be offered to the innocent people on the streets of Iran. This is the job of the United Nations, yet Ban Ki-Moon has been no stronger in his call to action than you have. Mr. President, you must push the U.N. on this. It is a human rights issue, and if Ban Ki-Moon is following your lead, it is imperative to remind him of the very charter of the U.N. to promote peace, freedom, and "reaffirm faith in fundamental human rights."

2. The United States cannot recognize the fraudulent elections of June 12, 2009. Mahmoud Ahmadenejad is not the elected president, and for the United States to respond to him as such gives further strength to Khamenei's dictatorship.

3. Mr. President, you must take this opportunity to evaluate your team of advisors on Iran policy. In this country we literally have the best and brightest academic minds from Iran. These are people who were born in Iran, who have a clear understanding of the complex workings of its political structure, its history, and its cultural nuances. With all due respect, I suspect that among the members of your team you have those with very distinct political agendas when it comes to the outcome of the Islamic Republic's future in the world. You must take a look and leverage those in this country who are capable of being neutral in respect in religion

and past politics. I urge you to surround yourself with some of the great minds you have right here in the United States who are qualified to advise you in the best possible way.

In closing, President Obama, I ask from the bottom of my heart that you recognize the blood on the streets of Iran as a problem not for Iran and not for the United States, but as a problem for our humanity. We cannot dance around these issues and when asked to respond chalk them up to not wanting to "meddle" with Iran's internal processes. We are all watching how you support the Iranian people, Mr. President. Iranians outside and inside Iran watch. Residents of the United States watch, and I, Mr. President, as someone who supported your march to the White House, wait and watch to see how you help support democracy and freedom for the people of Iran.

In remembrance of all those who have given their lives for peace, freedom, and democracy, I remain forever grateful,

Reza Mohajerinejad

What is striking to me about the difference between the protests in 1999 and those today is that in many ways, having Ahmadinejad represent Iran for more than four years now has brought average Iranians out in force. Similar to the U.S. citizens who were embarrassed at being represented by their president for eight long years during the Bush administration, Iranians have become weary of being associated with the likes of Ahmadinejad.

In July 1999, people came out into the street at a huge cost to their lives. Not only did they risk personal safety, but they could be blackballed by the government, their families could lose their jobs, and they could lose everything financially at the hands of the government. At that time, for the most part, only students were willing to gamble that much loss. A decade later, all bets are off. The general populous believes it is a fight worth stepping up for, and they will risk it all for freedom.

Ten years ago there was a great divide between our belief that change had to happen all at once and the reformists who wanted a phased approach to change. We wanted a new government from the ground up, with a real constitution and a true secular democracy for Iran. Our contemporaries at the time, Khatami's reformists, believed that change could happen gradually. They believed that the government could stay an Islamic-based institution, and that small steps could be taken toward a more progressive government.

The last ten years have changed the thinking of many of them. The masses are no longer comfortable having their government represented by Ahmadinejad. They were ready to stand up publicly and say to the world, "This is not our president." The candidates who challenged the incumbent began addressing students, women, and the Labor movement. They promised to fix the economic mess that Ahmadinejad swore to address, but only made worse in his first four years in office. They reached out to the students, understanding their power should they choose to support a candidate. In Iran there are close to three million student votes to gain, and winning their hearts and minds can literally decide an election.

It wasn't until the last three weeks of campaigning that Mousavi and Karroubi started to gain momentum. Support for candidates who were in opposition to Ahmadinejad was a demonstration by the masses that they were voting in opposition to the Supreme Leader, Ali Khamanei. While Mousavi proved to be the favorite among voters, in truth they were simply voting for the opposite of Khamanei's choice.

Following the disappointing election results, the protesters who came out demonstrated that a decade before, we had been right. Change needed to occur at the cellular level, and a new Iran needed to be built. Young people who were interviewed by foreign media before the government demanded they all leave said into the cameras that they were not so much followers of Mousavi, but proponents of freedom.

The election couldn't have come at a more emotional time—just weeks before the tenth anniversary of July 1999. Even though protesters were beaten and forced back into their homes, they came back out the week of the anniversary to make their voices heard. What reformists both inside and outside of Iran hoped would happen, for young and old alike to come out in remembrance of 18 Tir, proved not to disappoint. During demonstrations, at least ten students were killed by the Basiji thugs. Yet, for the most part, the demonstrations have remained nonviolent on the opposition side. Iranians have shown unity with one another, and put aside their differences to oppose the regime.

Outside of Iran there have been challenges in bringing people together for the cause, but more than any other time in the last thirty years, unity has been more common than infighting. While at some demonstrations there may be differences about which flag should be present, at the end of the day, for the most part, we have put down our individual platforms and spoken up for those inside Iran.

One of the most prevalent images since the election has been the color of resistance for the movement, a choice by Mousavi that has grown into a sea of green at virtually every demonstration. In truth, Mousavi presented the color as part of Shia Islam. The color green, however, has been taken back by the opposition. The origin of the color green within Persian culture can be traced back to the color of spring and new beginnings in Zoroastrian tradition and Nowrouz to Ferdowsi's Shahnameh, where green represents prosperity in nature. Mir-Hossein Mousavi chose green as his campaign color, but it has since become the symbolic color for opposition to the 2009 Iranian election results. Green is representative of a movement in which people lost their lives for freedom.

At present, the situation in Iran is still very much in flux. The demonstrations continue, and the violence toward them has not lessened. There have been forced confessions and a number of reformist leaders have been jailed. Many political prisoners have been executed or used as pawns by the Islamic regime to discourage more protests. Now, more than any other time, Iranians must unify if we are going to have change in our country. What has happened in these last ten years has proven beyond a doubt that the Islamic Republic of Iran must change. We knew it a decade ago, but there were those who didn't believe us at that time. Ten years later, the general populous in Iran knows it as well. That is a very big step. Finally, after the protests following the elections, the world knows it too.

Iran is no longer a vaguely understood country in the Middle East. It is no longer classified in the same category as Iraq and Afghanistan. That we are a progressive culture that consists of educated people in search of freedom and democracy has never before been so apparent to the West. The image that Ahmadinejad portrayed to the world has not held up. In many ways, he has been good for Iran in what he has done to bring awareness to the oppression people inside our country face. His fanaticism has backfired and made him and the regime look ridiculous. I believe before this is all said and done, the world will know unequivocally that Ahmadinejad is not representative of our country or our culture. That he and the rest of the theocrats have to go has never been more apparent to the world, but again, it has to come from inside Iran with support from those of us who are outside the country.

To make this change, however, the protests must continue. Protest has always worked in our history, and it will work now. It must be continued by all inside Iran—the students, the workers, the women, young, old, and all who want freedom. Additionally, workers must use their power to bring the country to its knees. They must find strategic ways to cripple the government. This is particularly difficult, as it may cause more strife for the people inside the country, but it is part of the sacrifice that we must endure.

The women's movement and the student movement must continue to work together. Women in Iran have more power today than ever. The universities are full of female students, and their bravery is unquestionable. They must push for a secular government to achieve democracy. Even those inside Iran who are deeply religious are weary of losing sons and daughters in the name of religion. They understand the need for a government that supports growth and freedom for its people. They need to continue to join forces with one another and come out in larger numbers so that the regime is overpowered by their response. The more people who come out, the less likely it is that the government can use their violence to control the masses. Additionally, there is great financial pressure put on the regime to employ the number of security forces it takes to control the masses who do not back down from protest. There is great power in numbers and persistence. Boycott the regime wherever possible, and find strategic ways to not follow rules. The system is at a breaking point, and the more we challenge processes that don't work, the closer we get to pushing the government over the edge.

As for those of us outside of Iran, at no time in our past has it been more crucial that we set our differences aside and unite for Iran. The answer to the end of the Islamic Republic of Iran will likely have to be another revolution. That is a simple truth. What kind of revolution depends on the people of Iran and how the current regime responds. To date, their reactions have been extreme violence. As they increase the use of violence against their own citizens, the history of our country shows that the reaction to that violence will likely have to be equally as forceful. Additionally, the regime has too much to lose to give up easily. The mullahs have accumulated a level of wealth that they try to hold on to at any cost. In a sane world we would all rather see a peaceful revolution where a new government could evolve and grow in a nonviolent way. This may not be possible with this regime. This is a simple fact, and one that we all must face. That said, our support from the outside will require financial assistance as well as working together to help in whatever the outcome is. We must also use media resources outside of Iran in support of those fighting for freedom inside Iran.

As I write this, I can scarcely believe that ten years have passed since 18 Tir, but then in some ways, it seems a lifetime ago. We were so young and idealistic at that time, and I am very proud to have been a part of the movement in those early days. I believe that we had something more than blind courage, though there was plenty of that. I believe we had a kind of knowledge that was beyond our years. If I really consider it, I would have to say that we called upon our history, and from that ancient time we gained strength to stand up to the oppression of the Islamic Republic.

In a recent speech at Friday prayers, Chairman of the Guardian Council Ahmad Jannati made a statement to the court that if they had killed the organizers of the student protests of 1999, today the Islamic regime wouldn't be facing the same problems. To Jannati I would say, as one of those organizers, if you had killed us, others would have stepped up. Maybe not that same day, that same month, or that same year, but the young generation would eventually have stood up against the theocratic dictatorship of the regime. They could have killed all of us, and they can kill those who have come after us, but they cannot silence the voice of freedom. It will not be quieted by simply killing its leaders. In fact, with every drop of Iranian blood that is spilled, the sound of freedom will become louder.

Today, I live in the Bay Area of California. I have managed to return to school, where I have had to go backward in order to move forward. Much of the political science I study I have lived in my political work for Iran. I have faced the violence of a dictatorship, and I have lived through a history that many of my classmates have only read about.

The other day, as I drove across the San Francisco-Oakland Bay Bridge, I was noticing the other people in their cars. A pretty safe assumption is that most of us crossing the San Francisco Bay were not hungry, wondering where our next meal was coming from. Most of us likely had opportunities to work, to earn a living, to drive on safe roads, and to live in relative freedom of expression. For the most part, no one on that bridge was concerned that they could be arrested that day, or that they might disappear for months or years and be tortured simply for their beliefs. This is what I want for the people of my own country.

I want for Iran a world where people don't live in fear of their government. I want children to grow up and know their true history. I want young people to be able to go to school and learn without the fear of oppression from a religious theocracy that robs them of their futures and steals the profits from our country's rich natural resources. I want a secular, democratic government for Iran. I want to return to my home in Babol. I want to smell the salt air as it blows in from the Caspian Sea. I want my country to be free.

# ABOUT THE AUTHORS

Reza Mohajerinejad is a student activist and one of the organizers of the Iranian student uprisings in July 1999—referred to according to the Iranian calendar as 18 Tir.

He founded the International Alliance of Iranian Students and the Global Student Alliance. He is a student at San Francisco State University.

Liz Malon is a freelance writer and political activist in the San Francisco Bay Area.

# REFERENCES

AntiWar.com. The best source for anti-war news, viewpoints, and activities. Potter, Gareth. "How the Neocons Sabotaged Iran's Help on al-Qaeda." http://www.antiwar.com/orig/porter. php?articleid=8590.

Gilbert, David. 2002. *SDS/WUO, Students For A Democratic Society And The Weather Underground Organization*. Montreal: Abraham Guillen Press & Arm the Spirit.

Kinzer, Stephen. 2008, 2003. All *the Shah's Men: An American Coup and the Roots of Middle East Terror*. Hoboken: John Wiley & Sons, Inc.

Parsa, Misagh. 1989. *Social Origins of the Iranian Revolution*. New Jersey: Rutgers, The State University.

Park, Mi. 2008. *Democracy and Social Change: A History of South Korean Student Movements, 1980-2000*. Oxford. Peter Lang Publishing.

Zhao, Dingxin. 2001. *The Power of Tiananmen: State-Society Relations and the 1989 Beijing Student Movement*. Chicago: University of Chicago Press.

Salam Iran. Constitution of the Islamic Republic of Iran.. http://www. salamiran.org/IranInfo/State/Constitution/.

"Silent No More. An Iranian student protester, sentenced to death for appearing on our cover, has escaped to America." *The Economist.* July 10, 2008.

SourceMex Economic News & Analysis on Mexico (Magazine/Journal). "Documents Confirm Government Role in Tlatelolco Massacre in 1968." 2003. Latin American Data Base/Latin American Institute